When the Family Gathers

Published by
LONGSTREET PRESS, INC.
A subsidiary of Cox Newspapers,
A subsidiary of Cox Enterprises, Inc.
2140 Newmarket Parkway
Suite 118
Marietta, GA 30067

Printed in the United States of America
1st printing 1996
Library of Congress Catalog Card Number: 96-76506
ISBN 1-56352-288-8

Cover art by Gayle Brainard
Jacket and book design by Jill Dible

When the Family Gathers

An International Cookbook and Calendar

Compiled and Written by Beverlie Reilman
FOREWORD BY ROSALYNN CARTER

Longstreet Press, Inc.
Atlanta, Georgia

CONTENTS

FOREWORD

Dear Friends,

It has been 19 exciting years since Jimmy first announced The Friendship Force, a cultural exchange program for families and, indeed, whole communities. Since that time, over half a million people in more than 50 nations have experienced Friendship Force magic: the joy of newfound friends and the feeling of belonging to a global family.

Since 1977, I have seen this wonderful organization "sow the seeds of friendship across the barriers that separate us." In fact, nine members of the extended Carter clan have traveled as ambassadors! I ardently support people-to-people diplomacy and believe that with knowledge and understanding, ordinary citizens hold the key to achieving the peace on earth we all desire.

Celebrate with us the rich diversity of our world's people through the traditional recipes that follow. Sample the unique flavors of dozens of countries and get a glimpse of life beyond our own borders. Meet our members, share our special memories, and become yourself a part of the wide world of The Friendship Force.

Rosalynn Carter

Rosalynn Carter
Honorary Chairperson of The Friendship Force

Former President Jimmy Carter and his wife, Rosalynn Carter, Honorary Chairperson of The Friendship Force since its introduction by President Carter in 1977.

INTRODUCTION

Participation in The Friendship Force sharpens the palate and introduces members to a variety of cuisine — from the daily fare of ordinary people to fancy and exotic company dishes. It's part of the fun of spending a week in the bosom of a host family.

Friendship Force travelers always return home with a recipe or two; one ambassador left the South Pacific with three versions of her particular fancy, Pavlova, from host family cookbooks in New Zealand and Australia. What fun to look forward to testing and tasting that delectable dessert in one's own kitchen!

In Gelsenkirchen, Germany, another member learned the value of menu simplicity during his week with a working-class family. Among the memories to take home was the morning walk with 10-year-old Suzanne to select warm *brötchen* from a tall basket at the corner grocery. What a delightful way to begin the day: hard-crusted, soft-centered fresh rolls covered with real butter, jam, or a thick slice of salami — or dipped into a soft-boiled egg nestled in a generations-old eggcup.

An Asian visitor to middle America was astonished to learn about the strange practice of everyone bringing a dish to a potluck supper — and to learn that all the plates went into the trash afterwards!

Sharing recipes and family practices are an important part of a Friendship Force exchange visit. Volunteer committees in each of the two partner cities seek to enlist adventurous people interested in exploring new cultures. Each weeklong visit opens the world so wide that ambassador members return home dedicated to hosting again and again — or traveling anew to share another intriguing lifestyle. They keep in touch through letters and the recipes they exchange.

When making preparations to host, families learn more about their own area's special foods, as well as local history and customs to show to new international friends.

Since 1977 over 125,000 ambassadors have learned to appreciate the unique culture of host families during more than 3,000 group visits. Today, in 53 countries on all continents except Antarctica, 358 Friendship Force clubs organize visits to assigned partners and host visitors from others.

When the Family Gathers presents a fantasy trip — through a calendar year of holidays and foods — to nearly 50 Friendship Force countries and 10 American regions.

Wayne Smith, president and founder of The Friendship Force, invites members and friends to spend each Tuesday night's dinner hour meeting a new country or region — by sharing the same meal with just plain folks in nations that circle the globe. Hopefully, the holiday calendar will help to make the world smaller, even as our organization has made friends around the world in the 19 years since its beginning.

A NOTE ON THE RECIPES

When the Family Gathers is a compilation of everyday recipes from the family files of Friendship Force members in almost 50 countries and 10 U.S. regions. The recipes are not intended to represent gourmet cooking.

Most ingredients listed in international recipes can be found in the largest American groceries. Others are available at a farmers market, an international market featuring foods from many nations, or at specialty stores which focus on Mexican and Spanish, Middle-Eastern, Asian, or other ethnic foods.

For uniformity, all international recipes have been converted to American measurements. However, recipes remain authentic as presented by Friendship Force members around the world. To return any recipe to metric measurments, please refer to the charts on pages 163-164.

The number of servings are not always included for desserts, breads, and appetizers, since serving sizes are variable. Main dish and vegetable recipes will serve from 4 to 6 persons, unless recipes specify otherwise.

FRIENDSHIP CAKE

1 cup greetings
1 to 2 cups smiles
2 large handshakes
2 or 3 cups love
1 teaspoon sympathy
2 cups hospitality

Cream greetings and smiles together. Then add handshakes beaten separately. Add love, slowly. Sift sympathy and hospitality and fold in carefully. Serve to your family and friends.

Sylvia Miller
Bird-in Hand, Pennsylvania

Part of the fun of getting together at a Friendship Force conference, festival, or exchange visit is the sharing of favorite foods. Six members who contributed recipes to this cookbook are pictured doing just that. From left to right are the following: Father Jorge Diaz of San Christobal, Mexico; Elizabeth Arthur of Accra, Ghana: Manfred Ketschker of Halle-Saale, Germany; Martin Cobbaert of Brussels-Pajot, Belgium; Noreen McLachlan of Hamilton, New Zealand; and Suzette Smissaert of Middleburg, the Netherlands.

The Friendship Force
57 Forsyth Street Northwest
Suite 900
Atlanta, Georgia 30303 U.S.A.

BEFORE THE FAMILY GATHERS

THE SELKIRK GRACE BY ROBERT BURNS, SCOTLAND

Some hae meat, and canna eat,
And some wad eat that want it,
But we hae meat and we can eat,
And sae the Lord be thankit.

A JEWISH BLESSING

Blessed is the Lord our God, Ruler of the universe,
who causes bread to come forth from the earth.

JAPANESE GRACES BEFORE AND AFTER A MEAL

Itadakimasu. (We are ready to eat.
We thank the farmer who makes this rice.)

Gochisosama. (It was a feast! Thank you!)

A TURKISH BLESSING

Afiyet Olsun. (May this food be pleasing to you.)

A MEXICAN GRACE

Señor, doy gracias por estos alimentos que nos has dado
ami y mi familia. En nombre del Padre, del Hijo y Espirito Santo.
(Bless us, O Lord, and these Thy gifts which we are about to receive
from Thy bounty through the Father, the Son and the Holy Spirit. Amen.)

AN OLD IRISH BLESSING

May there always be work for your hands to do;
May your purse always hold a coin or two;
May the sun always shine on your windowpane;
May a rainbow be certain to follow each rain;
May the hand of a friend always be near you.
May God fill your heart with gladness to cheer you.

Pork Chops and Mango Sauce

JAPAN

1st Week of January
NEW YEAR'S DAY

The most important festival in Japan, O-shogatsu, celebrates the new year from January 1 through January 3, when business is suspended and families reunite. New Year's Eve is the time to return home, prepare special holiday foods, clean houses, and decorate entryways with pine needles, bamboo stems, and sacred straw festoons.

Piles of dome-shaped rice cakes (*mochi*) are displayed — some embellished with dried kettlefish, seaweed, and Mandarin oranges — when the family gathers to share the happiness of good health and wishes for the coming year. As triumphant temple bells ring out the old year, the new one is welcomed by eating Toshikoshi Soba, "year-end" noodles of buckwheat which signify long life.

On New Year's Day most Japanese wear the traditional obi-sashed kimono — brightly colored and long-sleeved for young women; more subdued for older ones; dark and somber for men. At the larger Shinto shrines and Buddhist temples, where families pray for health and prosperity, long lines wind through the manicured grounds.

At home, sake (rice wine) is poured and Japanese songs of old are played on the *koto*, a long-stringed instrument of paulownia wood with a beautiful harp-like sound. Gifts of Otoshidama (New Year's money), are given to the children. Greeting cards are delivered to family members and friends.

For the traditional New Year's dishes of Zoni and Osechi Ryori, each ingredient has a symbolic meaning. Zoni is a fish soup, while Osechi Ryori are an assortment of special dishes eaten throughout the first days of the new year. Tiered lacquer

Noriko Nakamura pours Otoso, a special rice wine served in small tiered laquer cups on New Year's Day to assure health and happiness.

boxes are loaded abundantly with these multi-hued side dishes — which can be grilled, steamed, boiled, deep-fried, or vinegared.

Each is charged with good wishes: Tai (sea bream or snapper) is auspicious; Kazunoko indicates prosperity for one's descendants because herring roe have over 50,000 eggs apiece. Kobumaki, or Sea Tangle Roll, represents *yorokobu*, meaning happiness. Since the early 17th century, candied dried sardines have been offered to assure a rich harvest.

Taste, fragrance, color, and the four seasons are highly valued in the presentation of delicate Japanese cooking. Ingredients are chosen at their peak; the shape and type of serving pieces are selected in keeping with the season.

ZONI
(Fish Soup)

It is a Japanese tradition to begin the New Year meal with a special soup made from the yellowtail fish, which represents success, and the broth of flying fish because they are energetic and cheerful. The eight main ingredients in Zoni reflect the belief that eight is a good number and increases prosperity.

4 yellowtail fillets, each 2 ounces or more (or snapper,
   shrimp, salmon, or white chicken meat)
1 carrot
4 taro or Satoimo potatoes
4 Shiitake mushrooms
4 pieces dried kelp
1 bundle (3 ounces) katsuona leaves (or spinach)
4 cod fish cakes, sliced
4 cups flying fish broth (or chicken broth)
1 teaspoon salt
2 teaspoons soy sauce
2 teaspoons sake (rice wine)
4 round rice cakes

Cut yellowtail into bite-size pieces, boil for 2 to 3 minutes and discard broth. Prepare vegetables: cut 8 thin slices of carrot with a flower-shaped cutter and cook; pare the skin from taro, cut into bite-size pieces, and boil until soft; boil katsuona lightly, squeeze out the water, and cut into 1-inch lengths.

Make a broth by cooking a small flying fish (discard the fish) or use chicken broth; add salt, soy sauce, sake, and all ingredients except rice cakes. Simmer for 2 to 3 minutes. Grill rice cakes until they are lightly browned and swelled. Place one cake in each individual serving bowl and pour soup over each. Serves 4.

Noriko Nakamura
Fukuoka, Japan

OSECHI RYORI

KUROMAME
(Black Soybeans)

Wash 1 1/2 cups black soybeans (or black beans) and combine with 6 cups boiling water and 1/2 teaspoon salt. Set aside to soak overnight. Next day, boil the swelled soybeans and juice. Remove the cover often to add water; beans always must be covered by water. When the beans can be crushed between two fingers, add 1 3/4 cups sugar and boil for 4 or 5 minutes more. Set aside overnight, making sure beans are fully underwater. On the third day, boil again and add 1/2 teaspoon soy sauce.

TATSUKURI
(Dried Sardines)

Spread 2 ounces small, dried sardines on an oven sheet and heat in a moderate oven (350° F) for 80 to 90 seconds, until they are easily broken. In a saucepan, combine 3 teaspoons sugar, 2 teaspoons soy sauce and 2 teaspoons sweet sake (mirin). Heat for 2 1/2 minutes until thickened. Quickly blend with the sardines and spread on the oven sheet. Heat again, then sprinkle with white sesame seeds while still hot.

KAZUNOKO
(Herring Roe)

Remove salt from the herring roe by steeping in cool water, replacing the water 2 or 3 times. When salt is removed, drain and wash the roe. Remove the soft filmy skin and moisture from the surface and tear into bite-size pieces. In a saucepan, mix 3 teaspoons thin soy sauce, 2 teaspoons sweet sake (mirin), and 1/2 cup water. Add a few pieces of shaved dried bonito fish. Boil for 2 to 3 minutes and remove from heat; the shaved bonitos will sink to the bottom. With a spoon or small sieve, skim residue from the top. Cool and pour 2 or 3 teaspoons over the herring roe. Kuzunoko will keep for several days in the refrigerator by adding 2 or 3 teaspoons sake (rice wine) to the sauce.

Other Osechi Ryori are Crucian Carp boiled with soy sauce and sugar; Sweet Chestnut; Pickled Radish, salted and chopped with carrot; and Rolled Omelet.

Shinryu Akita
Shizuoka, Japan

Osechi Ryori, the traditional New Year's dishes in Japan.

CHAWAN MUSHI
(Egg Custard with Chicken and Shrimp)

3 eggs
1/2 cup tempura sauce
1 1/2 cups water
2 teaspoons sake (rice wine)
3 ounces chicken breast, skinned and boned
1 teaspoon soy sauce
8 spinach leaves, cut into 1-inch strips
8 shrimp, peeled and deveined
8 canned and boiled ginkgo nuts (Ginnan) or
    water chestnuts, drained

Beat eggs in a mixing bowl. Add tempura sauce, water, and 1 teaspoon sake, mix well, and put through a strainer; set aside. Cut chicken into bite-size pieces; sprinkle with soy sauce and remaining 1 teaspoon sake.

Combine chicken, spinach, shrimp, and nuts and place into 4 individual heat-proof cups. Slowly pour the egg mixture over the chicken and shrimp. Cover each cup with plastic wrap. Arrange cups in a large pot and add hot water to one-third the height of the cups. Cover pot and bring to a boil. Reduce heat

immediately and simmer for 15 to 20 minutes — until a skewer inserted in the center of each cup brings out clear broth. Or, gently shake each cup; if the custard is firm, it is ready.

Note: A substitute for tempura sauce is chicken broth with 1/2 teaspoon salt added.

Toko Yomura
Tokyo, Japan

KINTON
(Sweet Potato and Chestnut Cream)

1 or 2 sweet potatoes, enough to make 1 cup mashed
2/3 cup sugar
1/2 teaspoon salt
1 can (10 ounces) chestnuts

Peel sweet potatoes and cut into 1-inch lengths. Soak in water for 30 minutes. Bring water to boil and cook for 30 to 40 minutes or until very tender. Drain in a colander. Return sweet potatoes to the saucepot and mash them. Add sugar, salt, and the chestnuts in their juice. Heat again over a low flame for 5 to 10 minutes. Serve with other Osechi Ryori.

Toko Yomura

COLOMBIA

2nd Week of January
DAY OF KINGS
(La Llegada de Los Reyes Magos)

For the 95 percent of Colombians who are Catholic, the end of the Christmas season comes with fanfare on January 6, the Day of Kings, also known as Epiphany, the day on which Christians believe the Magi arrived in Bethlehem to pay homage to the Christ Child.

Colombians dress elegantly for Mass and the family dinner which follows. After a large and joyous meal, gifts are exchanged — perhaps on a smaller scale than at Christmas — with the giver saying solemnly: "The three wise men left this present at my house!" The remainder of the day might be spent with family photo albums, card games, and folk music. Aguardiente, a drink made from sugarcane, is popular on this occasion, as is Agua de Panela, an after-dinner libation of brown sugar and water, served like tea with milk or lemon.

Colombian families also celebrate Labor Day on May 1; Independence Day on July 20 to honor the new republic of 1819; victory over the Spanish at the Battle of Boyaca on August 7, 1810; and Columbus Day on the weekend closest to October 12.

Carnivals honoring various saints give a festive air to many communities throughout the year. Colombians living near the Atlantic seacoast of this country, which faces two oceans, flock to Cartagena on November 11 to salute with glorious fun the day in 1811 when the city drove out Spanish conquerors.

CHULETAS DE CERDO EN SALSA DE MANGO

(Pork Chops in Mango Sauce)

5 or 6 pork chops
2 small onions, chopped
3 cloves garlic, crushed
Juice of 2 bitter oranges (or mix of lime and
    grapefruit juice)
1 tablespoon oil
1/4 teaspoon pepper and salt to taste
2 small or 1 large egg, beaten
Flour to coat chops and oil
3/4 cup beef broth
Thyme, bay leaf, grated onion to taste
1/4 cup red wine

Francisco Gamboa experiments with the Colombian recipes of his family in Cali.

Marinate pork overnight in a mixture of the next 5 ingredients. To cook, dip each chop in beaten egg, dust with flour, brown in oil, and place in a baking dish. Season beef broth with desired seasonings and pour over the chops. Add wine, cover, and bake in a preheated 350° F oven for 30 minutes or until done. Serve with Mango Sauce. Serves 5 or 6.

Mango Sauce

3 ripe mangoes, peeled
1 large onion, chopped
5 cloves garlic, crushed
1 cup water
2 teaspoons sugar
3/4 teaspoon cinnamon
Lime juice to taste
3 whole cloves
1/4 cup vinegar
Pinch of black pepper
1/2 teaspoon beef bouillon granules or 1/2 cube
1 tablespoon margarine

Cut slices from the peeled mangoes. Combine pulp and pits with the next 7 ingredients and cook until mangoes are soft. Discard the pits. Place the remaining cooked mixture in a blender and process. Return to the pot, add other ingredients, and cook until thickened. Adjust seasonings to taste. Serve hot over pork chops.

Alvaro Gamboa
Cali, Colombia

Arroz con Cola a la Colombiana
(White Rice with Cola)

1 cup small-grained white rice
2 to 3 cloves garlic, halved
1 Cebolla Larga onion or 3 shallots, thickly sliced

2 to 3 tablespoons corn oil
2 1/2 cups dark cola
1/2 cup raisins, soaked in cola (above)
1 teaspoon salt in 1/4 cup water

Wash rice in a sieve until water runs clear. Drain. In a saucepan, fry garlic and onion slices for 2 to 3 minutes in oil. Add drained rice and stir over medium heat until rice is thoroughly coated with oil. Add cola and raisins, reduce heat to low, and cook uncovered until liquid is absorbed and bubbles appear. Pour salted water over the rice, but do not stir. Cover and continue cooking on low heat until the rice is tender and well cooked. Before serving, remove onion and garlic slices. Fluff rice well with a fork to keep it from compacting. Serves 4.

Cuqui Ardila
Bogota, Colombia

Lemon Custard Pie

Combine 1 cup heavy cream, 1 can (14 ounces) sweetened condensed milk, the juice of 3 lemons or limes (about 1/2 cup), and 1 envelope instant powdered lemonade. Process in a blender. Add 1 envelope unflavored gelatin and mix again. Pour into a graham cracker crust in a round 8-inch pie plate (or 4 individual tart shells), and refrigerate. Or use 4 tall goblets. Before serving, decorate with thin half slices of lemon or lime. Serves 4.

Maria Elena Rosero
Cali, Colombia

Pork chops with mango sauce.

PAPAS CHORREADAS
(Potatoes in Sauce)

6 medium boiling potatoes

1 tablespoon margarine

3 green onions, cut into 1-inch strips

2 tomatoes, peeled and diced

1/2 cup mozzarella or other white cheese, grated

1 cup milk

Salt and pepper to taste

Peel a strip around the middle of each potato and cook in boiling water until tender. In a small skillet, melt margarine and add onion and tomato. Cook until tender and add cheese, milk, salt, and pepper. Continue to cook, stirring, until cheese melts and the sauce thickens. Pour over potatoes. Serves 4.

Francisco Gamboa
Atlanta, Georgia

INDIA

Two important holidays begin the new year in India. Another in late October or early November seeks prosperity for the year to come. Each occasion is a time for family members to rejoice together.

The first, the Hindu feast of Makar Sankranti on January 14, marks the change of seasons, when the sun moves to its northern home and nights are shorter. Families visit temples or join in bathing rites in a holy river, the most sacred being the juncture of the Ganges and Yamuna. An old custom is to greet visitors with handfuls of sesame seed, saying "Eat sweetly, speak sweetly" to banish quarreling. Khichdi is a popular food.

Sankranti is also known as Kite Day. Skies are filled with colorful creations, especially in Gujarat, where kite stalls cover the streets with vibrant reds, blues, and yellows. People watch from rooftops as the night sky glitters with fighting kites to the cries of their jubilant fliers.

Later in January, Republic Day on the 26th includes a military parade in each state. In Delhi, a long caravan of children, military units, exotic floats, and festooned elephants winds through the capital while jet fighters scream overhead.

Perhaps the most important family day in India is Diwali, the festival of lights late in the year, when homes are cleaned and surrounded with earthen lamps filled with oil, candles, or perhaps electric bulbs. Sitting before a home altar, the eldest leads the family in a ceremony of worship for Lakshmi, goddess of wealth and prosperity. Then the sparkling lights are lit and the family shares a meal or refreshments. Gift-giving predominates throughout this holiday season.

In a country where each caste has different customs, diets vary as well. Wheat bread called *roti* is a staple in the north, while rice takes precedence in southern regions. Since many Indians are vegetarians, the cooking of vegetables has become a fine art. The popular and famous curry is meatless but also can be made with eggs, fish, meat, or poultry. Natives claim that the hot and spicy reputation of Indian dishes is exaggerated and believe that the flavors and pungency lead to better digestion.

KHICHDI
(Vegetable and Lentil Biryani)

2 pounds mixed vegetables: peas, potatoes, carrots,
  and green beans
1 3/4 cups white, long-grain rice
3/4 cup green split lentils, optional
2 tablespoons oil
1/4 teaspoon mustard seeds
3 dried red chilies
1/2 inch fresh ginger, crushed
1/4 teaspoon turmeric powder
Salt to taste
Coriander leaves to garnish
3 cups water

Wash and cut vegetables into small pieces. Combine, wash, and soak rice and lentils, in enough water to cover, for 30 minutes just before cooking. Heat oil in a heavy-bottomed skillet with a lid. Add mustard seeds and red chilies. When the mustard seeds begin to crackle, add the vegetables. Over medium heat, cook for 3 minutes, stirring continuously to prevent burning. Drain the soaked rice and lentils and add to the pan, along with ginger, turmeric, and salt. Stir well to mix. Add water, cover, and cook over low heat.

When the rice is cooked and vegetables are tender, turn into a serving bowl. Garnish with coriander leaves and serve hot. Serves 4.

Pulin Trivedi
New Delhi, India

RAITA

(Vegetables in Yogurt)

16 ounces plain yogurt
Salt and black pepper to taste
2 medium tomatoes, diced and drained
2 medium onions, finely diced
1 capsicum bell pepper, seeded and finely chopped
1/2 teaspoon cumin seed powder
Garnish: several coriander leaves and mint leaves,
    chopped

In a mixing bowl, add salt and pepper to yogurt and beat until smooth. Add all other ingredients except garnish and mix well. Turn into a serving bowl, decorate with garnish and serve cold with hot Khichdi or Chicken Curry. Serves 4.

Pulin Trivedi

CHICKEN CURRY

4 to 6 tablespoons vegetable oil
2 whole cloves
1/4 inch whole cinnamon stick
1 whole cardamon
1 bay leaf
2 medium onions, finely chopped

2 or 3 cloves garlic, ground
1/6 teaspoon turmeric powder
Red chili powder or paprika to taste
Salt to taste
Hot water, as directed
8 chicken drumsticks, skinned
1/4 cup tomato purée
1/4 inch fresh ginger, grated
Ground cumin and black pepper
Cilantro to garnish

In a large heavy skillet or wok, heat oil and add cloves, cinnamon, cardamon, and bay leaf. Stir and add onions. Cook a few minutes, until the onions turn golden brown, stirring often. Add garlic and cook for a few seconds until golden but not burned. Add turmeric, chili powder, salt, and 2 tablespoons hot water. Stir, cook for 10 minutes, and add — 2 table-spoons at a time — 1 cup hot water. Mixture should be smooth and paste-like.

Add chicken pieces and tomato purée, stirring. When the mixture begins to dry and the oil to separate, add 1/2 cup hot water a tablespoon at a time, as needed, and cook for another 10 to 15 minutes.

Finally, add 2 more cups hot water and grated ginger. Reduce to low heat, cover, and cook for 10 to 15 minutes

Raita, a yogurt dish with tomatoes and onions, goes well with finely chopped fresh vegetables.

Jogi Singh offers Chicken Curry, one of her family's favorites in New Delhi.

until the chicken is tender. Remove cloves, cinnamon, cardamon, and bay leaf. Sprinkle with cumin and black pepper and turn heat to warm. After 20 to 30 minutes, transfer to a serving dish and sprinkle with cilantro. Serve with basmati rice and a green salad. Yield: 4 servings.

Jogi Singh
New Delhi, India

JALEBI

(An Indian Sweet)

1/2 cup self-rising flour
Pinch of baking powder
6 tablespoons water
1/2 cup yogurt
Ghee (clarified butter) for deep frying

SYRUP
1 cup sugar
1 cup water
1/2 teaspoon saffron
Milk
2 teaspoons rose water, if desired, for flavor

GARNISH
1/2 teaspoon cardamon powder
1 tablespoon pistachios, blanched and sliced
Red rose petals (optional)

Sift flour and baking powder. Add water to yogurt, beat well, and combine with the flour to form a thick batter of pouring consistency. Set aside. To make the syrup, dissolve the sugar in water and boil for 5 minutes. Warm the saffron in a small vessel, add a little milk, and rub until the saffron dissolves. Add saffron and rose water to the syrup. Set aside but keep warm.

Heat the clarified butter in a nonstick frying pan. Select a plastic bottle and make a small hole no larger than 1/4 inch in diameter in the lid. Fill with batter and squeeze from the bottle into the hot clarified butter, forming a pretzel shape. Fry each "pretzel" on both sides until golden brown. Drain and drop the fried Jalebi into the hot sugar syrup. Leave for 2 minutes to absorb the syrup, then remove and arrange on a plate. Sprinkle garnish over the Jalebi.

Pulin Trivedi
New Delhi, India

SCOTLAND

4th Week of January
BURNS' NIGHT

The birthday of revered poet Robert Burns on January 25 — known as Burns' Night to Scots the world over — evokes romanticism and Scottish nationalism, which ran especially high in 1996, the 200th anniversary of Burns' death.

Since the 1707 union of Scotland and England, feelings for independence agitate from time to time, but never more so than on Burns' Night.

Traditionally the meal must be Haggis, a simple peasant's dish that perfectly fits any celebration of the "Ploughman Poet," although a beef course or fish from the sea or lakes of Scotland — salmon, smoked haddock, or fried herring — might also be present.

Beginning with the poet's Selkirk Grace (see page X), the ritual for Burns' Night never varies. A bagpiper salutes the haggis as it comes to table, born aloft on a silver platter or bricklayer's hod. An honored guest recites Burns' "To a Haggis" as the "great chieftain o' the pudding race" is pierced with an ornamental knife or sword. Speeches are followed by toasts of whiskey, another famous Scot.

Haggis — in truth, a sheep sausage — is a mixture of oatmeal, liver and other parts of lamb, onions, suet and seasonings, originally simmered in a sheep's stomach. No longer made at home, it is available in butcher shops ready for the kettle. Neeps and Chappit Tatties always accompany Haggis — Neeps is short for large yellow-fleshed Swedish turnips and Tatties are potatoes to be "chapped" or mashed. Burns' Night dinners begin with the traditional Cock-a-Leekie Soup and end with Scotch Trifle or bannocks and cheese.

All in all, it's a fitting meal for the man who gave the world "Auld Lang Syne"!

HAGGIS, NEEPS, AND CHAPPIT TATTIES

1 haggis
4 or more mild Swedish turnips (or rutabagas), peeled and cut into bite-size pieces
4 tablespoons (1/4 cup) butter
Salt and pepper
4 or more potatoes, peeled and cut into bite-size pieces
2 tablespoons milk

Place haggis in a kettle, cover with boiling water, and simmer for 45 minutes. Meanwhile, simmer turnips in lightly salted water for 30 minutes; drain and mash until smooth, adding 2 tablespoons butter and pepper to taste. Keep warm. Likewise simmer the potatoes in lightly salted water for 20 minutes; drain and mash until smooth. Heat milk, add to the potatoes with remaining butter, and beat until creamed. Transfer the cooked haggis to a platter and arrange the potatoes and turnips around it.

Edna Twivey
Strathaven, Scotland

HAGGIS-IN-A-BOWL

Since an authentic Haggis may be available in America only at a Scottish or English food shop in areas where a Burns Club exists, Haggis-in-a-Bowl offers an acceptable substitute for Burns' Night.

Over low heat, lightly brown 2 cups dry rolled oats and set aside. Mince 4 medium onions and sauté until transparent. Mince 2 cups boiled lamb's liver to a pâté consistency. Combine oats, onions, liver, salt, and pepper plus any other desired seasonings, such as parsley and Jamaica allspice. Chop a piece of suet and add, along with enough stock from boiling the liver (or beef broth), to moisten the mixture.

Form into a firm rounded oval shape, similar to meatloaf, and place into a baking bag. Loosely tie the bag and place on a rack in a baking pan. Add water to the level of the rack, cover and steam in a moderate 350° F oven for 30 to 45 minutes. Drizzle single-malt Scotch whiskey over it and serve on a platter with Neeps and Tatties.

Michaele Finegan
Raleigh, North Carolina

COCK-A-LEEKIE SOUP

In a kettle, cover a small chicken with chicken stock (or stock cubes in water). Add seasonings to taste (salt, pepper, parsley, allspice, and a pinch of sugar). Cover and simmer until the chicken falls apart, for 2 hours or more. Add 8 leeks, finely chopped, during the last 45 minutes. Remove the chicken and reserve for another meal. Strain the broth and serve very hot.

Edna Twivey

CRANACHAN WITH BANNOCKS
(Fruit Cream and Oatcakes)

CRANACHAN
3/4 cup rolled oats
1 cup chilled heavy cream
2 1/2 tablespoons sugar
2 tablespoons Scotch whiskey or Drambuie (or 2
teaspoons vanilla)

1 to 2 cups fresh sliced strawberries, diced peaches,
raspberries, blackberries, or a combination

In a dry skillet, toast oats for a few minutes over medium heat, stirring. Whip cream until soft peaks form; continue whipping and slowly add sugar and Scotch. When the cream is thick, fold in the toasted oats, fruit and a bit of juice to color the cream and add flavor. Serve with bannocks or oatmeal cookies.

BANNOCKS
1 7/8 cups rolled oats, divided
1/4 cup flour
1/2 teaspoon baking powder
1/4 teaspoon salt
1 tablespoon sugar
2 tablespoons shortening
1/4 cup hot water or more

Process oats in a blender to a coarse flour. Set aside 3/8 cup. Mix remaining 1 1/2 cups with all-purpose flour, baking powder, salt, and sugar. Melt shortening, add water, and stir into the dry ingredients. Dough must be stiff; if needed, add water a tablespoon at a time. Knead on a lightly floured surface until well mixed. Roll out dough to 1/8-inch thickness. Sprinkle remaining oats and press onto the dough. Cut rounds with a cookie cutter, or form a circle and cut farls (wedges). Bake on an ungreased cookie sheet in a 350° F oven until lightly browned.

Michaele Finegan

AUSTRALIA
5th Week of January
AUSTRALIA DAY

There is nothing Australians enjoy more on a day free from work than to get together with their mates and family for a real Aussie barbecue. Coming in the middle of a hot summer, Australia Day beckons most families to the backyard or to a recreation area. Others observe flag raisings, often to a roll call representing Australia's diverse heritage, or citizenship ceremonies, toasts to Her Majesty the Queen, sports contests, or cultural events that focus on the reason for the January 26th holiday.

Australia Day salutes those who pioneered the country more than 200 years ago and those who preserved its freedom. On January 26, 1788, Captain Arthur Philip led the first European settlement ashore at Sydney Cove. Beginning as a penal colony, melding with natives already there and enriched by generations of immigrants, Australia has reason to celebrate those first settlers, who cooked their salted beef and a bread called damper on open wood fires as they built a nation out of bush.

Today, in addition to barbecue, a hearty slice of Australian Meat Pie topped with tomato sauce, steamed peas, and buttered damper recall the food which sustained the early settlers in the outback. A vase of kangaroo paw or bottle brush flowers and checked tablecloths continue the ritual. Old bush ballads by the Bushwhackers Band would complete the picture of earlier times.

Any meal on Australia Day is likely to produce authentic Australian desserts: Peach Melba or Pavlova, a meringue dessert topped with strawberries and cream. Or Anzac biscuits — named for the Australia and New Zealand Army Corps — which were sent by women from "down under" to their soldiers in both world wars.

AUSTRALIAN MEAT PIE

FILLING

1 tablespoon vegetable oil

2 onions, sliced

2 1/4 pounds blade steak or chuck roast, cut into
    1-inch cubes

1/2 cup water

1 bacon stock or beef bouillon cube, crumbled

1 teaspoon salt, optional

1/2 teaspoon pepper

1 tablespoon beef gravy powder

2 tablespoons flour

1/4 cup water

PASTRY

1/4 to 1/2 pound (1/2 cup) butter or margarine

2 1/2 cups flour, sifted

1/2 teaspoon baking powder

1/2 teaspoon salt, optional

2 tablespoons water

1 tablespoon lemon juice

Milk for glazing

To make filling: Heat oil and cook onions until lightly browned. Add next 5 ingredients, cover, and simmer gently for 1 hour or until the meat is tender. Blend gravy powder and flour with water and add to the meat and juices to make gravy. Stir and cook for 2 minutes. Cool.

To make pastry: Rub butter into flour, baking powder, and salt; add enough combined water and lemon juice to form a firm dough. Knead lightly. Roll out 2/3 of the dough and line a 9-inch pie plate; spoon filling into the pastry shell and glaze the edges with milk. Roll out the remaining pastry, cover the filling, and seal the edges. Glaze with milk and make two slits in the top to allow steam to escape. Bake in a moderately hot oven at 450° F for 30 to 35 minutes, until pastry is golden brown. Serves 6.

Patricia Murray
Sydney, Australia

DAMPER

(Settlers' Bread)

2 cups self-rising flour
1/2 teaspoon salt
1 teaspoon sugar
2 tablespoons butter
3/4 cup milk

Sift flour and salt into a large bowl; stir in sugar. Rub in the butter until the mixture resembles fine bread crumbs. Add most of the milk at once and mix into a soft dough, adding remaining liquid if the dough is not soft enough. Place on a floured board and knead lightly. Pat the dough to form a low mound. Place on a greased oven tray and glaze with a little extra milk. Bake in a 480° F oven for 10 to 12

Australian Meat Pie is served with peas and fresh rolls.

minutes until golden brown.

To serve, slice 1/2-inch thick and spread with butter and golden syrup, maple syrup, corn syrup, or honey. Serves 6 to 8.

Jenny Vout
Newcastle, Australia

LAMB KEBABS

2 pounds boneless lamb, cut into 1 1/2-inch cubes
1/4 cup salad or olive oil
2 cloves garlic, crushed
1 small onion, finely chopped
3 tablespoons parsley
1/2 teaspoon marjoram
1/2 teaspoon thyme
Freshly ground black pepper
1 green and 1 red capsicum pepper (similar to bell pepper)

Skin and trim the lamb pieces. Marinate in remaining ingredients (except peppers) in a covered glass or earthenware bowl for 4 to 8 hours in the refrigerater, turning meat occasionally. Before cooking, bring meat to room temperature.

Seed peppers and cut into 11/2-inch wedges. Alternate lamb and peppers on skewers, brush with marinade, and grill over moderate heat for about 20 minutes, turning frequently. During cooking, baste with marinade. Serve with tossed salad and foil-baked potatoes. Serves 6 to 8.

Note: If kebabs are placed directly on an open grill, baste more often than if you put them on a cookie sheet or other hot plate.

Valerie Yakimoff
Newcastle, Australia

Jenny Vout's Damper harks back to pioneer days in the outback.

ANZAC BISCUITS

1 cup plain flour
1 cup rolled oats
1 cup coconut
1 cup sugar
Pinch of salt
8 tablespoons (1/2 cup) butter or margarine
1 tablespoon golden syrup or dark corn syrup
1 teaspoon baking soda
3 tablespoons boiling water

Combine the first 5 ingredients. Melt butter and syrup and add baking soda dissolved in boiling water. Stir into the dry ingredients and mix well. Place spoonfuls of dough onto a greased oven tray. Cook for 15 to 20 minutes in a moderately slow oven (325° F). The cookies should be removed when deep golden brown but still soft to the touch.

Gae Harris
Adelaide, Australia

PRAWN COCKTAIL

Shell and boil 1 1/2 to 2 pounds of prawns (or shrimp). Arrange a bed of shredded lettuce in each glass serving dish or sherbet glass. Add prawns, spoon Cocktail Sauce on top, and garnish the side of each dish with a lemon slice. Serve with two triangles of bread or toast.

COCKTAIL SAUCE

1 tablespoon tomato sauce
1/2 tablespoon Worcestershire sauce
2 tablespoons cream
3 tablespoons mayonnaise
Lemon juice to taste

Combine all ingredients and chill.

Dawn Woollard
Newcastle, Australia

The picnic table for Australia Day always features Damper.

Mountain States: Rocky Mountain High Hamburger Soup

MOUNTAIN STATES, U.S.A.

1st Week of February
APRÈS SKI
(An After-Skiing Party)

For American families living in the western mountain states, skiing is a way of life that provides growing-up memories to last forever and a reason to gather grandchildren together for their spring break from school. Downhill or cross-country skiing on a day trip from home, or sleigh rides and other winter fun from a vacation condominium, are ideal activities in Colorado, Idaho, Montana, Wyoming, and Utah.

The western mountains on both sides of the Continental Divide not only provide some of the most glorious American scenery, but also give a glimpse into the lives of native tribes and the hardships of pioneer settlers. Luxurious ski resorts are surrounded by abandoned mines, historic sites, and deserted boomtowns that tell the romantic story of how hard it was to win the West. But in the months from November through April, the ski runs get the

Barbara Dieter tosses her Wilted Spinach Salad.

most attention from Rocky Mountain families.

Après Ski, with a salute to the French, is a happy time to recharge batteries and recount the thrills and spills, adventures and misadventures, of the day. Food must be high-energy and nutritious but simple, easy to prepare, and quick, since the cook has been skiing, too! Ideal dishes would be those where everything is thrown into one pot; salads that are ready for a final tossing, or a cheese fondue which includes meat, vegetables, and bread chunks for dipping. A relish tray and crackers can stave off immediate hungers. Desserts are allowed to be rich and sweet, to restore energy. And tableware and decorations must be as informal as the skiers themselves!

CHEESE FONDUE

2 cloves garlic
3/4 cup light cream (half-and-half)
3/4 cup dry white wine
1 pound Swiss cheese, diced or grated
1/2 teaspoon dry mustard
1/4 teaspoon nutmeg
1 to 1 1/2 teaspoons seasoned salt
1/2 teaspoon pepper
1 tablespoon or more cornstarch

Rub the inside of a fondue pot with the cut sides of garlic cloves and set aside. In a saucepan over medium heat, combine cream and wine. Heat to just below boiling and gradually add a mixture of cheese and seasonings, stirring constantly. If too thin, remove 1/2 cup of the cheese mixture, slowly blend in cornstarch as needed, and return to the saucepan to thicken. Bring to

At an international Friendship Force conference, Diny Goossens of Holland (left) and Judy Elting of Colorado exchange their cook-book recipes.

a boil and transfer to a fondue pot, preheated on its warming stand.

To serve at table — with fondue forks, dip pieces of choice from the following: French bread chunks, ham cubes, hard sausage pieces, and fresh vegetables. Serves 4.

Barbara Dieter
Colorado Springs, Colorado

ROCKY MOUNTAIN HIGH HAMBURGER SOUP

1 pound lean ground beef or ground turkey
1/2 cup onion, chopped
Salt and pepper to taste
1/2 teaspoon cumin

2 cans (15 ounces each) Italian-style stewed tomatoes
2 cans (15 ounces each) beef broth
1 can (15 ounces each) green beans
1/2 cup uncooked bow-tie pasta or other egg noodles

In a large soup pot, brown the meat with onions and cook until onions are tender. Drain. Add remaining ingredients and bring to a boil. Reduce heat, cover, and simmer for 15 minutes. Yield: 4 dinner servings.

Don Reynolds
Colorado Springs, Colorado

WILTED SPINACH SALAD

2 tablespoons onion, finely chopped
1/4 teaspoon pepper
1/3 cup vinaigrette dressing
6 cups fresh spinach, torn into pieces
4 bacon slices, crisp and crumbled
1/3 cup Parmesan cheese, grated
1 hard-boiled egg, chopped

Combine onion, pepper, and vinaigrette dressing and heat without boiling. Combine spinach, bacon, and cheese. Toss with warm dressing and top with chopped egg. Serves 4 to 6.

Barbara Dieter

CHOCOLATE CHIP DATE CAKE

1 cup chopped dates
1 teaspoon baking soda
1 1/2 cups boiling water
1/2 cup shortening
1 cup sugar
2 eggs, beaten

1 1/4 cups plus 3 tablespoons flour
1/4 teaspoon salt
3/4 teaspoon baking soda
1 package (6 ounces) chocolate chips
1/2 cup sugar
1/2 cup chopped nuts
Whipped cream, sweetened

x 13″ pan and top with chocolate chips, sugar, and nuts. Bake in a 350° F oven for 40 to 45 minutes — less in high altitudes — or until the cake tests done. Serve with sweetened whipped cream.

Shelley Pruett
Colorado Springs, Colorado

Add 1 teaspoon soda to the dates; pour on boiling water and let the mixture cool. Cream shortening and sugar; stir in beaten eggs and add to the date mixture. Sift flour, salt, and 3/4 teaspoon soda and add to the mixture. Place in a greased and floured 9″

Spiced Wassail

3 oranges, studded with 16 cloves
6 cups apple juice
2 cups cranberry juice
1 teaspoon aromatic bitters
1 teaspoon whole allspice
6 sticks cinnamon
1 cup rum, if desired
Slices of 1 orange, studded with cloves

Heat oven to 350° F. Insert cloves into oranges and place in a shallow baking pan; bake for 30 minutes, piercing oranges several times with a fork. In a large saucepan combine juices, spices, cinnamon sticks, and oranges. Simmer for 20 minutes (oranges should fall apart), add rum, and bring to a boil. Discard cinnamon sticks and oranges. Pour into a heat-proof punch bowl and add fresh orange slices studded with cloves. Serve hot. Yield: 16 half-cup servings.

Judy Elting
Littleton, Colorado

Dessert Fondue Sauces

Caramel Fondue Au Rum

3 tablespoons butter
1 1/2 cups firmly packed brown sugar
1/2 cup evaporated milk
2 tablespoons rum or 1 teaspoon rum extract

In a medium saucepan, melt butter over low heat. Stir in brown sugar and, gradually, the milk. Continue stirring until the sugar dissolves. Remove from heat and let stand for 3 minutes. Stir in rum and serve warm. Yield: 1 1/2 cups.

Chocolate Fondue

2 ounces (2 squares) unsweetened chocolate
1 tablespoon margarine or butter
1 cup sugar
Pinch of salt
1 teaspoon vanilla
2/3 cup evaporated milk

In a small saucepan, melt chocolate and butter over low heat. Stir in sugar, salt, vanilla, and, gradually, the milk. Heat and stir until sugar dissolves.

Jan Elting
Littleton, Colorado

Dippers for Dessert Fondues

Cubes of angel food or sponge cake
Vanilla wafers or ladyfingers
Large marshmellows
Fruits: orange or tangerine sections; banana,
*   apple or pear slices; pineapple chunks; strawberries*
*   or other berries*

SINGAPORE

2nd Week of February
CHINESE NEW YEAR
(Chin Jie)

The beginning of the Lunar New Year signifies for Singapore Chinese another fresh start in one's life, fresh hopes for happiness and prosperity. Chin Jie is not only 15 days of fanfare and merrymaking but also a time to renew family ties, to forgive, and to look forward to the future. Gifts are exchanged; red packets containing money (*hongbao*) are given to children, unmarried relatives, and friends. *Kum* are oranges which visitors bring to symbolize wealth and good fortune.

By long tradition, the eve of the New Year holiday is Reunion Day for the Chinese family, the cornerstone of their society. The home is thoroughly cleaned and decorated profusely: red drapes over the entrance welcome the New Year with the color of life; sugarcane denotes thanksgiving; potted plants of fruit and pussy willow are decorated with red fish shapes and tiny lanterns to call forth good fortune.

Spring couplets on red paper strips are hung everywhere, each bearing an inscription in Chinese characters, such as "May you gaze upon happiness when you open the door!"

The head of the family hosts the Reunion Dinner as members gather from far and near. Respect and love flow freely between parents and children, between young and old.

The main dish will be Yusheng, the raw fish salad which is symbolically tossed high by eager hands to begin the meal. Side dishes might be Baked Chicken, Prawns in Plum Sauce, Steamed Sea Bass, Broccoli

Before tossing, Raw Fish Salad makes a pretty table in Singapore.

Members of The Friendship Force in Singapore toss Yusheng.

Stems in Oyster Sauce, and the Happy Harmony, a delicious assortment of delicacies. Au Nee is a traditional dessert made of sweet yams, pumpkin, and gingko nuts.

YUSHENG
(Raw Fish Salad)

FRESH INGREDIENTS:

2 small carrots or 2/3 cup, shredded

2 long green radishes, (or horseradishes) shredded

2 long white radishes, shredded

1/2 orange, pomelo, or grapefruit, seeded and sectioned

Juice of 2 limes or 1 lemon

1 tablespoon each: Chinese parsley and spring onion shreds

1/2 tablespoon each: shreds of chili, lemon leaf, and young ginger

6 to 8 ounces fish fillet — dorab, salmon, or red carp

1/2 cup jellyfish shreds

PICKLED, PRESERVED, AND DRY INGREDIENTS:

1/4 cup cooked peanut oil

1/2 cup plum sauce

1/2 teaspoon each: powdered cinnamon and ground pepper

2/3 cup toasted peanuts, ground

1/4 cup sesame seeds, dry roasted or lightly fried

2 tablespoons each: shreds of white pickled ginger, red sweet preserved ginger, preserved leek and preserved nutmeg

1 1/2 tablespoons each: shreds of preserved melon and lime

2 tablespoons crispy, fried sliced shallots

1 tablespoon mandarin orange peel

2 tablespoons sweet cucumber pickle shreds

2 1/2 to 3 cups crispy pretzels or crackers

RAW FISH SALAD, SIGNIFYING ABUNDANCE (YU) AND LIFE (SHENG), HAS A SPECIAL STATUS DURING LUNAR NEW YEAR THAT IS UNIQUE TO SINGAPORE CHINESE. IT CONTAINS ABOUT 30 DIFFERENT INGREDIENTS — FRESH, PRESERVED, PICKLED, SWEET, SOUR, CRISPY, AND FRIED — AND ITS COMBINED FLAVORS RANGE FROM SWEET TO SHARP, FROM TART TO SPICY. TEXTURES VARY FROM SOFT AND SMOOTH TO CRUNCHY AND GRITTY. WITH CHOPSTICKS, EVERYONE AT THE FAMILY TABLE JOINS IN TOSSING THE SALAD AS HIGH AS POSSIBLE TO GATHER WEALTH, PROSPERITY, AND GOOD FORTUNE.

Separately, soak finely shredded carrot and radishes for 1 hour. Squeeze out excess water and dry on a piece of cloth. Set aside on individual plates. Remove scales and debone the fish fillets. Refrigerate for 3 hours. Cut fillets into thin slices, add a drizzle of vegetable oil, pepper, and lime or lemon juice, and mix well.

To toss the salad: Mix peanut oil and plum sauce in a large bowl or serving platter and place fish meats on top. Sprinkle cinnamon and pepper, ground peanuts and sesame seeds over the fish. Add the fresh shredded vegetables and the remaining fresh, pickled, and preserved ingredients. Add crushed pretzels or crackers. Raw Fish Salad is now ready for tossing.

Jane Kee, Jessie Lee, Audrey Lum,
Elsie Chia, and Alice Phua
Singapore

BAKED CHICKEN WITH STUFFING

3- to 4-pound chicken

1 cup oil

2 cloves garlic, chopped

1 onion, chopped

1/4 pound lean pork, cut into small cubes

1 chicken liver, cubed

3 Chinese or button mushrooms (stems removed),
    soaked and diced

1 small turnip (peeled, salted, and soaked in water 1
    hour, then squeezed and cubed) or 1/4 cup black
    salted turnip, soaked and cubed

2 each: fresh and boiled water chestnuts, skinned and
    diced (optional)

2 dried lotus leaves, boiled

1 sheet of strong paper used for baking

2 sheets of aluminum foil

SEASONING MIXTURE FOR CHICKEN

2 teaspoons each: salt and fine sugar

2 teaspoons each: dark and light soy sauce

3 tablespoons water

2 teaspoons cooking wine

GRAVY

1/2 teaspoon salt

1 1/2 teaspoons each: sesame oil, fine sugar, and light
    soy sauce

Pepper to taste

1 tablespoon cornstarch mixed with 5 tablespoons
    water

Clean the chicken, rub inside and out with seasoning mixture (stirred well) and marinate for at least 1
hour. In a saucepan, heat oil and brown the marinated chicken until golden. Set aside to cool. Leaving
only 2 1/2 tablespoons of oil in the pan, fry garlic and
onion. Add pork and chicken liver cubes, mushrooms, turnip cubes, and nuts. Stir well. Add the
gravy seasonings, well mixed. Stir and thicken with
the cornstarch mixture. Set aside to cool.

Stuff chicken with the cooked ingredients. Wrap
in lotus leaves, followed by baking paper and then
aluminum foil. Bake for 45 minutes in a preheated
350° F oven. Lower temperature to 250° F and bake
for another 45 minutes or until the chicken is tender.

To serve, place wrapped chicken on a serving
plate. Open wrapping and fold up edges to form a
bowl to retain heat and the gravy. Serve hot.

Jane Kee, Jessie Lee, Audrey Lum,
Elsie Chia, and Alice Phua

Baked Chicken with Stuffing is a favorite in Singapore.

INDONESIA

3rd Week of February
LEBARAN

On August 17, 1995, Indonesia celebrated the 50th anniversary of its independence from Dutch colonial rule. In the intervening years since the end of World War II, this Asian country of 13,000 islands strung along the equator has become an independent nation boasting strong economic and social development.

While Independence Day is important to Indonesians, the holiday closest to their hearts is Lebaran, a Muslim feast coming at the end of Ramadan, the ninth month of Islam's lunar calendar, which is dedicated to fasting. Almost 90 percent of Indonesians are Muslims, who consider themselves cleansed and reborn after the fasting. For Lebaran — or Hari Raya in Malaysian — family members return to their hometowns to greet relatives and ask forgiveness of one another; children kneel before parents to receive their blessing.

After morning prayer at a nearby mosque, dressed in their finest new clothing, the family gathers at the home of the eldest among them to feast on many delicacies prepared during the previous days. Food trays are exchanged with neighbors, as are handshakes and acts of forgiveness. Later, parks, zoos, and amusement centers offer their own inducements.

The favorite foods of these islanders are the national rice dish, Nasi Goreng; a popular salad, Gado-Gado; charcoal-roasted meats called Sate; and displays of fruit — mangos, bananas, papayas, and grapes. A variety of Indonesian, Chinese, Indian, and Western dishes are also popular, always with steaming heaps of fluffy white rice.

Although Indonesia's complex blend of ethnic groups numbers 336, for the Muslims celebrating Lebaran, just as for all Indonesians saluting Independence Day, they become one group of happy, thankful people.

Marinated beef or shrimp are skewered on bamboo sticks and grilled to make Sate.

SATE
(Marinated Meat or Shrimp)

MARINADE FOR CHICKEN SATE

2 tablespoons soy sauce

1 1/2 teaspoons tamarind juice

3 tablespoons vegetable oil, warmed

1/2 teaspoon coriander

MARINADE FOR BEEF SATE

2 tablespoons vegetable oil, warmed

1/2 teaspoon salt

1 teaspoon lemon or lime juice

2 tablespoons soy sauce

MARINADE FOR SHRIMP SATE

2 tablespoons melted margarine

1 clove garlic, chopped

1 teaspoon salt

1 tablespoon soy sauce

1 tablespoon tamarind juice

MARINADE FOR PORK SATE

2 tablespoons peanut oil

2 candlenuts, grated

2 tablespoons sweet soy sauce

1 clove garlic, chopped

*1 teaspoon shrimp paste, softened in 2 tablespoons
   warm water*

MARINADE FOR LAMB SATE

2 tablespoons vegetable oil, warmed

1 tablespoon soy sauce

1 small onion, grated

*1/2 teaspoon shrimp paste, softened in 2 tablespoons
   warm water*

2 cloves garlic, chopped

For cocktails or as an entrée, select one or more: 2 chicken breasts; 1 pound of beef tenderloin; 1 pound large fresh shrimp; or boneless lean pork or lamb. Cut meats into bite-size portions and thread on bamboo sticks, using a different skewer for each type of meat or shrimp. (Metal skewers are not recommended, as they would adversely affect the taste.)

Mix together the appropriate marinade, coat the meat, and let stand for 2 hours — for shrimp, marinate for only 1 hour. Place skewers on a charcoal grill until well done but not dry, basting as necessary. If desired, serve with Gado-Gado Peanut Sauce (below).

Friendship Force Board Members
Jakarta, Indonesia

GADO-GADO WITH PEANUT SAUCE
(Indonesian Salad)

1 bean curd or tofu cake, cut into pieces

1 teaspoon vegetable oil

1 small cabbage, chopped and parboiled

1/2 pound fresh bean sprouts

1/2 pound spinach, parboiled

*1/2 pound green beans, cut in halves, or 1 can cut
   beans, drained*

1 bunch watercress, parboiled

1 cucumber, sliced

2 or 3 sliced carrots, cooked but still crisp

2 eggs, cooked and sliced

Fry bean curd in oil until brown, and prepare vegetables. Place bean curd, vegetables, and egg slices on a large platter, separately or mixed together. Serve with Gado-Gado Peanut Sauce.

GADO-GADO PEANUT SAUCE

1 tablespoon vegetable oil

1/2 cup onion, chopped

1 clove garlic, chopped

4 tablespoons crunchy peanut butter

1/2 cup water

3 green chilies, crushed

1 small stem lemon grass

1 teaspoon brown sugar

1/8 teaspoon shrimp paste

1 tablespoon tamarind juice

1 teaspoon soy sauce

1/2 teaspoon salt

1/2 cup coconut milk

Fry onions and garlic in oil and set aside. Mix peanut butter with water and bring to a boil. Remove from heat and add other ingredients except coconut milk. Combine with onions and garlic and mix well.

Three generations of an Indonesian family begin Lebaran with morning prayer at the mosque.

Stir in coconut milk until smooth and simmer over low heat for about 1 minute. For a spicier sauce, add more chilies. Serves 4 to 6.

Friendship Force Board Members

NASI GORENG
(Fried Rice)

*2 cups long-grain rice (cooked with 2 teaspoons salt in
    2 1/2 cups water)*
2 cups chicken or pork, diced
2 tablespoons vegetable oil
1 large white or yellow onion, sliced
1 large red onion, chopped
2 cloves garlic, chopped
1/2 teaspoon coriander
1/2 teaspoon laos (a type of ginger)
1/8 teaspoon shrimp paste
1 red chili pepper, crushed
2 tablespoons sweet soy sauce
1 cup cooked shrimp

Cook rice and set aside. Fry the meat in oil until light brown. Add onions and garlic and cook until brown. Lower heat and add coriander, laos, shrimp paste, and pepper. Mix well and fry for 1 minute. Add soy sauce and shrimp and mix well. Add the cooked rice, stirring constantly until the rice turns light brown.

Keep warm while making a thin omelette: whip 1 egg, 1/2 teaspoon salt, and 1/8 teaspoon pepper; fry in a large nonstick pan, flipping over once. Remove and cut into long strips. Garnish the rice with omelette strips or, if desired, thin cucumber slices placed around the edges.

Friendship Force Board Members

Gado-Gado is an Indonesian salad served with peanut sauce.

ESTONIA

4th Week of February
INDEPENDENCE DAY
(Eesti Iseseisvuspaev)

Because of recent history, Independence Day in Estonia has become a day of quiet remembrance, thanksgiving, and sharing within the family circle — a way to express love for the country other than showy parades. The holiday commemorates February 24, 1920, when, after centuries of oppressive foreign influence, independence from Russia was first gained. Until 1940, the rich Estonian folk heritage with national costumes and a mother tongue flourished. Today, in spite of 50 enforced years as part of the Soviet Union, their unique culture thrives once again.

In this far north Baltic nation, winters are extreme and summers are welcome. The most important holidays — outside of Independence Day — coincide with the winter and summer solstices. Jōulud (Christmas) marks the end of darkness, and Jaanipaev, or Midsummer, celebrates the longest day of the year. Estonia also is known for colorful song and dance festivals, where folk costumes of gay colors and intricate embroidery are common among the celebrants.

Although Independence Day is likely to be spent with a quiet family gathering at home, the midsummer festival in June is more social and is usually celebrated around cookfires out-of-doors, eating roasted meat, ash-baked potatoes, and picnic fare.

To supplement the roasted meats, there might be rye pies (two circles of dough with meat, potato, and mushroom filling), boiled eggs, cheese scones, or sandwiches of rye bread and caraway cheese. Thirsts might be quenched by honey beer, juniper berry tea, or one of many varieties of home-brewed barley malt beer.

Folk songs add to the festivity, and young people compete for the longest jump across the fire. It's midsummer, after all, and the longest day seems to last forever!

Melenie Dickinson of California greets old friends Ene Seene and Hugo Alas of Tallinn, Estonia.

HAPUKAPSAS SEALIHAGA
(Estonian Sauerkraut)

2 pounds sauerkraut, homemade or canned
1 pound pork, cubed, or pork chops
1 medium onion, chopped and sautéed in oil
1/2 cup pearl barley, washed
Water
1 teaspoon each: salt and sugar

Place sauerkraut and pork cubes in a casserole, stir in sautéed onions, and sprinkle the washed barley on top. Add enough water to cover and season

Estonian Sauerkraut includes pork, onions, and pearl barley.

with salt and sugar. Cook in a moderate oven (350° F) until the pork is tender. Season with salt and sugar. If pork chops are used, place them on top of the sauerkraut. With cubed pork, Estonian Sauerkraut can be cooked in a kettle on the stove instead of in the oven. Serve with potatoes and a green vegetable.

Imbi-Reet Kaasik
Tallinn, Estonia

KLIMBISUPP
(Meat Soup with Dumplings)

1 pound beef, cubed

3 quarts water

2 carrots, sliced

2 small onions, diced

1/4 cup parsley

Salt to taste

5 medium potatoes, diced

DUMPLINGS

6 tablespoons butter

1 egg yolk

Salt to taste

2/3 cup hot broth or milk

1 cup flour

1 egg white, beaten

Place cubed beef and water in a saucepan and bring to a boil. Skim off the foam and continue simmering at low heat. Add carrots, onion, and parsley.

Make the dumplings: combine the egg yolk with butter, add salt, broth, then flour, and mix well. Add the beaten egg white; the mixture should be rather firm.

When meat and vegetables are almost tender, add salt and potatoes. Drop dumplings from the end of a tablespoon and continue cooking until dumplings come to the surface and all ingredients are tender.

Imbi-Reet Kaasik

KARTULISALAT

(Potato Salad)

2 pounds potatoes, boiled

1/2 pound carrots, boiled

2 cucumbers, peeled, or equivalent amount sweet pickles

1/2 pound peas, lightly cooked unless canned

1 onion

2 or 3 hard-boiled eggs

1/2 pound cooked ham or sausage

1 medium apple

Spices to taste: salt, pepper, and dill

Mayonnaise

Sour cream

Prepare the main ingredients by cutting into 1/3-inch cubes. Add spices. Combine enough mayonnaise and sour cream to lightly cover all. Chill and serve with barbecued meat and sausages.

Ene Seene
Tallinn, Estonia

OTHER ESTONIAN SALADS

PEEDISALAT

(Beet and Caraway Salad)

Peel 6 medium beets and cut into thick slices. Cook until tender. Mix 1/2 cup sugar, 2 tablespoons vinegar, and 1/4 cup beet juice or water. Pour over beets and sprinkle with 1 teaspoon caraway seeds.

SEENESALAT

(Mushroom Salad)

Lightly cook 1/2 pound or more mushrooms, leaving the smaller ones whole and slicing the larger. Slice 2 small onions and add salt to taste. Mix mushrooms and onions together, then fold in 1/2 cup or more sour cream until vegetables are coated.

Hugo Alas
Tallinn, Estonia

Italy: Rita Levoni with her Peperonata

WALES

When you see a daffodil or leek worn on the lapel of a Welshman, even those far away from home, it is sure to be March 1, St. David's Day in this most Celtic of countries. The daffodil is the national flower, the leek its most popular symbol, and St. David is the patron saint of this land of natural beauty whose history goes back 1,200 years. The Welsh tongue still prevails here, as do over 400 castles in various degrees of ruin.

St. David was a missionary who founded 12 monasteries and the cathedral community in Pembrokeshire named for him, as are 50 churches in South Wales. He died on March 1 sometime in the sixth century. His life is celebrated in local schools with poetry readings and old Welsh tunes and tales. Young girls dress in the Welsh national costume from the 18th century; older students plan concerts and competitions in song, dance, and poetry.

Wales is noted for its many Eisteddfods, the music and dance festivals of which the most famous is the Royal National Eisteddfod, a week-long celebration of Welsh culture and the largest folk event in Europe. More than 30 festivals are held each year in this small country.

The Welsh family gathers on any convenient day close to March 1 to share a tableful of traditional Welsh food, with daffodils and small Welsh flags as the centerpiece. Some will serve mutton or lamb, as sheep farming and shearing are major industries. Leek soup is always present, as are Barabrith, a bread speckled with dried fruit soaked in tea; Welsh cakes, small scones cooked on a bakestone; a moist fruitcake known as Teisen Lap; and perhaps old peasant dishes such as Cockles and Welsh Rarebit. In Cardiff, the entire family might spend the evening at a Gymanfa Ganu, a festival of singing at St. David's Hall.

Croeso i Gymru! Welcome to Wales!

A TRADITIONAL WELSH BREAKFAST

IN DAYS GONE BY, WHEN THE MEN AND WOMEN OF WALES NEEDED A SUBSTANTIAL BREAKFAST TO SEE THEM TO WORK ON THE LAND OR DOWN IN THE MINE, THEY WOULD START THE DAY WITH A HOT BREAKFAST OF BOILED COCKLES, LAVER BREAD, AND WELSH BACON.

COCKLES ARE TASTY MOLLUSKS THAT LIVE IN THE SAND AROUND THE COAST OF WALES. ALSO FOUND GROWING ALONG THE COAST IS LAVER BREAD, A SEAWEED RICH IN VITAMINS AND MINERALS. AFTER BEING WASHED AT LEAST SIX TIMES AND COOKED FOR FOUR HOURS, IT IS TOSSED IN FINE OATMEAL IN SMALL FLAT CIRCULAR POTS AND FRIED WITH WELSH BACON. ALTHOUGH COCKLES AND LAVER BREAD ARE AVAILABLE IN TINS, THE MOST SATISFYING BREAKFAST RESULTS FROM THOSE GATHERED BY HAND OR FRESH FROM THE MARKET.

Barabrith Bread features dried fruits soaked overnight in tea.

BARABRITH
(Speckled Bread)

8 ounces mixed dried fruit, chopped
3/4 cup strong black tea
2 scant cups self-rising flour
1 teaspoon mixed spices (half cinnamon, half nutmeg)
1 scant cup soft brown sugar
1 egg
2 tablespoons water, as needed

Soak fruit in tea overnight. Next morning, combine all ingredients and stir well. Add water if needed to make a smooth, thick batter. Fold into a greased 1-pound loaf pan. Bake in a preheated 325°F oven for 1 hour and 15 minutes, until Barabrith tests done. Make thin slices and serve with butter or cream cheese.

Note: If using all-purpose flour, add 1/2 teaspoon salt and 1 teaspoon baking powder to each cup to make the equivalent of self-rising flour.

Margaret Heath
Cardiff, Wales

WELSH LAMB WITH HONEY

3- to 4-pound lamb (leg or shoulder)
1/2 teaspoon salt
1/2 teaspoon pepper
1 teaspoon ginger
2 tablespoons rosemary
8 ounces honey
1/2 pint apple cider

Line an ovenproof dish with foil. Rub the joint with salt, pepper, and ginger. Place it in the dish and sprinkle with half the rosemary. Cover the top with honey and pour cider around the meat. Begin cooking in a hot oven at 420° to 450° F. Allow 20 to 25 minutes per pound plus an additional 20 minutes. After the first 30 minutes, reduce to 400° F and add the remaining rosemary. Baste during cooking, adding more cider if necessary. Serve with seasonal fresh vegetables. Serves 6.

Margaret Lewis
Cardiff, Wales

TEISENNAU AFAL
(Apple Cakes)

3/4 cup butter
1/2 cup cooking fat or shortening
2 cups self-rising flour
3/4 cup sugar
1/2 teaspoon cinnamon
Pinch of salt
2 medium cooking apples, peeled and finely chopped
1 egg
Milk

Rub fats into the flour; add sugar, cinnamon, and salt. Add apple pieces, egg, and enough milk to form a stiff dough. Roll out and cut into small squares or rounds. Cook on a well-greased, moderately hot bakestone griddle or frying pan for 3 minutes on each side, until golden brown. Or spread into an ovenproof dish and bake at 375° F for 35 to 40 minutes. Cut into squares. May be sprinkled with sugar and eaten with warm Welsh butter.

Daphne Pavitt
Cardiff, Wales

CAWL CENNIN
(Potato and Leek Broth)

1 pound potatoes, peeled and sliced
1 pound white parts of leeks, sliced
Butter
3 cups milk
2 cups vegetable or chicken stock
Salt and pepper
1 cup light cream
Garnish: chopped parsley

Simmer potatoes and leeks in a shallow pan of water with a small lump of butter. When soft and water has boiled down — in 20 to 30 minutes — allow to cool and then liquidize in a blender or put through a sieve. Return to the pan, and add milk, stock, salt, and pepper; do not boil or the milk will curdle. Add cream and stir well. Serve in warm bowls and sprinkle with parsley. Serves 4 to 6.

Claire Hudson
Cardiff, Wales

SEWIN WITH CUCUMBER SAUCE

4 sewin (sea trout) cutlets or salmon steaks
Juice from 1 lemon

CUCUMBER SAUCE
1 small cucumber, peeled and diced
1 onion, finely chopped
2 tablespoons butter
1 cup chicken stock
1 teaspoon each: salt, pepper, and tarragon
2 tablespoons cornflour (cornstarch)
Milk

Sprinkle lemon juice over the fish and wrap in foil. Place in an ovenproof dish and cook in a moderate oven at 350° F for 30 minutes.

To make cucumber sauce: In a saucepan, cook the cucumber and onion in butter for a few minutes, until soft. Add stock and seasonings, simmer for 20 minutes, and then liquidize in a blender. Just before serving, reheat the sauce and thicken it with cornstarch mixed with a little milk, stirring until smooth. Pour over the fish and serve with creamed potatoes, carrots, and broccoli. Serves 4.

Daphne Pavitt
Cardiff, Wales

Potato and Leek Soup is popular and hearty when served with Barabrith.

ITALY

2nd Week of March
SAN GIUSEPPE
(St. Joseph's Day)

Although March 19, St. Joseph's Day, is not a civic holiday in Italy, it is an important time for families to gather. St. Joseph is universally celebrated as the protector of the Holy Family; in religious Italy his feast day has come to be the perfect day to honor all fathers. As in every country on Father's Day, the head of the house receives special gifts when the family meets to attend church together or to share a meal.

Wherever a church is dedicated to St. Joseph, the saint's statue is taken on the shoulders of four stalwart men and paraded through crowded streets. Often a civic band trails behind to offer folk and reverential songs. The stalls of church fairs present a colorful array of items from artisans who practice ancient crafts in remembrance of St. Joseph, a carpenter by trade. Throughout Italy, food and flower fairs brighten the early spring.

In Sicily, where St. Joseph is patron saint and gentle defender of the unfortunate, food-laden altars are built in the name of charity and entire villages partake in a procession to an outdoor banquet table piled with gifts from parishioners. A trio representing the Holy Family — perhaps an aged man, a young widow, and an orphan — receives the gifts on behalf of all the needy. The day ends with singing, dancing, and festive parades winding through the village squares, where communal bonfires help to give thanks to the humble saint who inspires this generosity. *Viva San Giuseppe!*

Although no particular food is traditional on St. Joseph's Day — except perhaps ring donuts called Zeppole di San Giuseppe — it may be that a favorite meal of the father of the house is the one the family chooses when they gather on March 19.

GNOCCHI DI PATATE AL FORMAGGIO
(Potato Dumplings and Cheese)

2 1/4 pounds potatoes
2 1/2 cups flour
1 egg
Salt to taste
7 ounces Piedmontese or Gorgonzola cheese, grated
Garnish: shredded Parmesan cheese, melted butter, and crushed garlic

Boil, peel, and very finely shred the potatoes. Add flour, egg, and salt, working all together to obtain a solid, soft dough. Roll into cylinders about 1/2 inch in diameter and cut into 1-inch-long pieces. Press with a floured fork, laying each aside briefly on a floured towel. Place the gnocchi in salted, boiling water until they float. Remove with a pierced ladle and place in serving dishes, cover with grated or diced cheese, and garnish with Parmesan, butter, and garlic. Serves 4.

Rita Levoni
Piacenza, Italy

PEPERONATA
(Pepper and Tomato Stew)

2 pounds red and yellow capsicum or bell peppers
1 pound ripe tomatoes
1/2 cup olive oil
1 onion, sliced
Basil leaves, to taste

Each potato dumpling is formed between a fork and the cook's thumb.

Cut capsicum peppers into halves and remove seeds, white filaments, and stems. Slice and wash them. Briefly dip tomatoes in boiling water, then remove skin and seeds and cut into pieces. In a kettle or frying pan, place olive oil, peppers, tomatoes, onion, and basil to taste. Cover and cook over low heat about 1 1/2 hours. Add salt and adjust the liquid to obtain a light sauce — add a little water if too dry; remove the cover and increase the heat if too thin.

Optional: Add desired amount of browned ground meat during the cooking process. Serves 4.

Rita Levoni

FRITTELLE

(Rice Balls)

1 heaping cup rice
2 cups milk
1/2 cup water
3/4 cup sugar
3 eggs
2 tablespoons butter, softened
1/2 cup soft orange candies, minced
Flour
Olive oil to fry

Cook rice with milk, water, and sugar. Cool, then add 2 eggs, butter, and the orange candy pieces. Shape dough into small balls, to the preferred size. Dip each ball, first in the remaining beaten egg, then in flour. Fry the frittelle in boiling olive oil.

Melina Maggini
Pisa, Italy

CIAMBELLA

(Ring Cake)

3/4 cup butter, melted and cooled
1 2/3 cups sugar
4 eggs
1/2 teaspoon salt
1/2 cup milk
4 cups flour
1/2 ounce (2 packets) yeast
1 teaspoon vanilla

Butter a springform pan and dust with flour. Place a 3-inch ovenproof glass (or cardboard cup) in the center. Preheat the oven to 375° F.

In a large bowl, blend butter with sugar, eggs, salt, milk, and flour combined with yeast. Add vanilla. Stir and mix well. Pour the dough into the ring-form mold and place it in the oven for 50 minutes without opening the door. Turn off the heat and let the cake remain in the oven an additional 5 minutes. Remove from the oven and open the outer rim of the spring-form pan to cool the cake. Serve Ciambella with a good Italian white wine.

Note: If desired, a bundt cake pan can be used; when the cake has cooled, turn it upside down onto a round cake plate.

Rita Levoni

IRELAND

3rd Week of March
ST. PATRICK'S DAY

Sure 'tis a great celebration around the emerald isle — and wherever Irishmen have roamed — when March 17 rolls around and it's St. Patrick's Day once again. In the land of the shamrock, thousands of people with Irish backgrounds join with native sons of Erin in riotous celebration of the simple fact that they are Irish.

Even if the weather turns foul, 400,000 Irish will line St. Stephen's Green for the annual parade in Dublin, and more will watch from warm and cozy pubs. There's lavish entertainment, marching band competitions, festivities, and fun throughout the land — and it lasts a full week!

The Irish who immigrated to America in the 19th century brought St. Patrick with them, and today American cities large and small copy Dublin's grand parade — in Paddy's honor or as an excuse to frolic — followed by jolly Irish fun 'til the day is done. New York City's parade is the largest. In Georgia, Savannah streets turn green with Irishmen pursuing its green beer, while half a million Atlantans watch a four-hour stream of bands and floats. Boston, perhaps the most Irish city, celebrates for two days.

Honored for introducing Christianity to Ireland, St. Patrick was born about A.D. 385 in Roman Wales. He escaped slavery in Ireland, studied in a French monastery, and returned to pagan Ireland as a missionary intent on conversions. Legend has it that the shamrock became the national emblem when St. Patrick used it to demonstrate the doctrine of the Holy Trinity. He died on March 17, 471, and is buried in his adopted homeland.

A St. Patrick's day celebration wouldn't be complete without Irish pub food, such as the famous Shepherd's Pie, Boxty, and Fadge. Boxty is a crepe filled with savory meats, and Fadge is a flat griddle bread. Irishmen also expect the traditional dense, brown soda breads, Dublin Bay prawns, smoked and fresh salmon, sea and brook trout, lamb, steaks, and hearty Irish stew of mutton and vegetables. These St. Patrick's Day favorites are washed down with boisterous songs and tall glasses of Guiness stout, poured slowly to settle the foam.

ST. PATRICK'S DAY CIDER CUP

Dip the rims of Irish crystal goblets 1/8 inch down into unbeaten egg white, then into green-colored fine sugar. Leave them to dry and set. Dice a mixture of prepared fruits — apples, pears, peeled plums, or other fruit in season (except those which are squashy or bleed their colors, such as red or black berries). Gooseberries, well prepared and blanched, help this colorful ensemble. Place fruit in the glasses and cover with cider. Chill and serve as a dinner course or, as an afternoon appetizer, with a wafer biscuit.

Angela Muckley
Bantry, Ireland

SMOKED SALMON CASSEROLE

2 tablespoons butter
1 pint cream
2 cloves of garlic or to taste, coarsely chopped
6 large potatoes, thinly sliced
1 medium side of smoked salmon, about 1 1/2 pounds
Garnish: lemon slices, chopped parsley

Melt butter in a saucepan; add cream, garlic, and

potato slices and simmer gently until potatoes are transparent. Line the bottom of a 2-quart casserole with potatoes and alternate with slices of smoked salmon until approximately four layers have been added, ending with salmon. Pour any remaining cream sauce over the top and cook uncovered in a 350° F oven for 15 to 20 minutes. Garnish with lemon slices and chopped parsley, and serve with a mixed green salad or steamed broccoli.

Angela Muckley

St. Patrick's Day Cider Cups complement Smoked Salmon Casserole.

BANTRY BAY FISH SOUP

6 tablespoons butter

1 onion, minced

1 1/2 pounds fillet of whiting or other mild whitefish

2 pints Bantry Bay mussels

1 small bunch parsley

2 pints light fish stock or hot water

6 slices bread, cubed and fried in butter

Salt and pepper

Melt 4 tablespoons of butter in a saucepan, add onions, and fry gently. Remove onions and keep hot. Fry the fish in the pan until it is brown and fully

cooked, about 5 minutes. Flake the fish and place with the onions in a hot bowl. In another pan, heat remaining 2 tablespoons of butter; when sizzling, add mussels and parsley. Fry for 5 minutes and add the fish stock. Cook until mussels open. Remove and discard parsley. Remove mussels, discard shells, and, with stock, add to the fish. Garnish with cubes of fried bread. Heat slowly and season with salt and pepper to taste or other seasonings of choice.

Angela Muckley

IRISH COFFEE

Cream: rich as an Irish brogue.
Coffee: strong as a friendly hand.
Sugar: sweet as the tongue of a rogue.
Whiskey: smooth as the wit of the land.

Heat a stemmed whiskey goblet. Pour in 1 shot of Irish whiskey — its smooth taste and full body add to the enjoyment. Add 1 teaspoon sugar. Fill the goblet with strong coffee to within 1 inch of the brim and stir to dissolve the sugar. Top with cream whipped lightly so that it floats on the coffee.

Do not stir again: the true flavor is obtained by drinking hot coffee and Irish whiskey through the coolness of the cream.

Angela Muckley

CRUBEEN PEA SOUP

15 ounces split green or other dried peas

2 crubeens (pig's feet) or substitute country ham hock
    or ham bone

3 1/2 pints cold water

1 celery stalk, chopped

1 ounce lentils, washed

Irish Coffee deserves its universal reputation.

Steep the peas overnight. Next day, scrub crubeens thoroughly. Put into a saucepan, add water, bring to a boil, and simmer gently until the meat begins to fall from the bone — at least 3 hours. Then add the drained peas, celery, and lentils and simmer for 1 more hour. When the soup is done, rub as much as possible through a sieve. Add any seasoning desired. Reheat and serve. Serves 6.

Angela Muckley

SHANGRI-LA BROWN SODA BREAD

4 teaspoons bread soda (baking soda)
6 heaping cups (2 pounds) wholemeal (whole wheat)
flour
2/3 cup brown sugar

Pinch of porridge oats (oatmeal)
1 cup pinhead oatmeal (fine-cut)
2 eggs
2 pints buttermilk

Sieve the soda and mix all dry ingredients. Make a well in the center of the dough and add eggs and milk. Mix thoroughly. Grease well four 1-pound loaf pans, divide the dough among them, and place in oven pre-heated to 375°– 400° F for 45 to 60 minutes, until crispy on top and tester comes out clean.

Angela Muckley

SOUTHWESTERN STATES, U.S.A.

4th Week of March
TEX-MEX BARBECUE

A mixture of languages and cultures greets visitors to the states which stretch across the lower boundary of the United States. Great expansive vistas offer a clue to the wide-open friendliness and informality of the citizens and their equal dedication to work and leisure.

Southwesterners see themselves as inheritors of a culture that has flowed back and forth across the Mexican border, enriched by the Indians and Spanish explorers who came first and by western expansion. Immigrants from other continents and transplanted Americans have added to the intriguing mix.

Since informality is the key, the popularity of barbecues, rodeos, and Tex-Mex food is not surprising. A barbecue feast of beef, pork, or chicken — slow-cooked with the sauce added in the last 15 minutes — can be thrown together any time family and friends gather in the backyard. Fajitas, enchiladas, tacos, cowboy beans, casseroles, and salads that include these and other staples are everyday fare to these folks. Tex-Mex counts on tortillas, pinto beans, cheese, and 2,000 different varieties of chilies to define this satisfying cuisine. In these beautiful and enchanting states, salsa has passed ketchup as the king of condiments.

Table coverings at a barbecue or gala picnic — especially on Cinco de Mayo, the Mexican holiday which is celebrated throughout the Southwest on May 5 — may be a red-and-white-check cloth, western bandanna, or Mexican serape. Bright crepe paper flowers, Indian pottery, and hurricane-lamp candles brighten the patio. Even high-tech urban professionals wear boots and jeans or colorful Mexican dress. The appropriate drinks are margaritas, made with limes and lemons from one's own trees, and tequila. Freshly churned ice cream, pralines, flan, and sheet cakes are fitting desserts.

SMOKY BEEF BRISKET

3- to 5-pound beef brisket
2 tablespoons liquid smoke
2 tablespoons Worcestershire sauce
Pepper, onion salt, garlic salt, and celery salt to taste

Cut excess fat from the beef brisket and pierce in various places with a knife point. Sprinkle liquid smoke, Worcestershire sauce, and seasonings over both sides of the meat and rub in. Wrap beef in heavy

Smoky Beef Brisket is the specialty of Kathie Slaughter.

foil and bake for 4 to 5 hours in a 250°–275° F oven, until the meat is tender and the thermometer reaches 170° F. Keep warm in foil until needed. Slice thinly against the grain and serve with meat juices on the side. It can also be served cold or reheated in the sauce or any barbecue sauce. Serves 8 to 10.

Kathie Slaughter
Las Vegas, Nevada

SOUR CREAM CHICKEN ENCHILADAS

1/2 cup cooking oil
12 corn tortillas
1 cup onion, finely chopped
2 cups longhorn Cheddar cheese, grated
2 cans cream of chicken soup
1 pint sour cream
1 1/2 cups cubed cooked chicken
1 can (4 ounces) green chilies, diced

Heat oil in a large skillet. Dip each tortilla a few seconds, until sizzling but still soft. Drain on paper towels. Place a little onion and grated cheese on each tortilla, roll, and place in a 9″ x 13″ baking dish. Combine soup, sour cream, chicken, chiles, and remaining onions. Heat, pour over tortilla rolls, and separate with a spatula to allow liquid under and around the tortillas. Top with the remaining grated cheese.

Heat for 20 to 25 minutes in a 350° F oven until the casserole is bubbling and the cheese is melted. Serve very hot with green salad, tomatoes, and jicama, or with refried beans. Serves 6.

Geneva Baldwin
Mesa, Arizona

FIESTA WEEK!

THE ETHNIC DIVERSITY OF THE SOUTHWESTERN STATES IS NEVER BETTER DISPLAYED THAN IN SAN ANTONIO, THE HOME OF THE ALAMO, WHEN BRASH, NOISY, AND COLORFUL FIESTA WEEK BEGINS AROUND APRIL 21 — THE DAY IN 1836 WHEN TEXAN SAM HOUSTON DEFEATED MEXICAN GENERAL SANTA ANA AT SAN JACINTO. THE BATTLE OF FLOWERS, RIVER PARADE, AND FLAMBEAU PROCESSION OF LIGHT AND COLOR ARE SPECTACULAR, THE HISTORICAL SIGNIFICANCE IS OVERWHELMING — AND IT IS VINTAGE TEX-MEX!

SONORA CASSEROLE

3 cups sliced zucchini, steamed until soft
1 cup corn, frozen or canned, drained
2 cups tomato sauce
1/2 tablespoon chili powder
1/4 teaspoon cayenne powder
1/4 teaspoon ground cumin
1 teaspoon vinegar
1 can (4 ounces) green chiles, diced
1 1/2 cups cheddar cheese, grated
1 cup sour cream
1 bunch green onions, chopped
6 corn tortillas, quartered and fried in oil

Preheat oven to 350° F. Mix all ingredients except the last four. Place in a casserole and top with cheese. Bake until cheese melts, for about 12 minutes, and serve hot. Top with sour cream, sprinkle with chopped green onions, and decorate by inserting tortilla quarters upright on the top. Serves 8 to 10.

As an appetizer, serve with extra tortillas and margaritas.

Ann Ayres
San Antonio, Texas

MEXICAN SHEET CAKE

2 cups sugar
2 cups flour
2 eggs
2 teaspoons baking soda
1 can (20 ounces) crushed pineapple, undrained
1 cup English walnuts, chopped

FROSTING
1/2 cup butter or margarine, softened
1 package (8 ounces) cream cheese, softened
2 cups powdered sugar
1 teaspoon vanilla

Mix all ingredients and pour into a 9″ x 13″ cake pan. Bake for 25 to 30 minutes in a 350° F oven until the cake tests done and is light brown. While the cake cools, prepare frosting: Beat butter and cream cheese until creamy. Add powdered sugar and vanilla and mix until smooth. Spread on the cooled cake.

Note: June Prade of San Antonio makes a similar cake but substitutes chopped bananas for half the pineapple.

Virginia Bliss
Austin, Texas

TEXAS CAVIAR

1 can white hominy, drained
2 cans black-eyed peas, drained, or 1 can each black-eyed peas and black beans
1 onion, chopped
1 small bell pepper, chopped
2 medium tomatoes, chopped
1 jalapeño pepper, chopped, or 1 can (4 ounces) green chilies
1/2 cup dried parsley
Minced garlic to taste
1 bottle (8 ounces) Italian dressing

Mix and chill to blend flavors. Serve with tortilla chips or crackers as an appetizer.

Renee Hermanson
San Antonio, Texas

Geneva Baldwin presents her Sour Cream Chicken Enchiladas.

Thailand: Coconut Pudding

RUSSIA

ORTHODOX EASTER

The English scholar St. Bede believed Easter was named for a Teutonic goddess of fertility; other ancients connected it with the spring equinox and the awakening of life after the darkness of winter. Whatever its festival origins, Easter remains the bedrock for all nations embracing Christianity. Preceded by 40 days of fasting and a holy week dedicated to the last journey of Christ, Easter bursts upon believers as a joyous day of awakening — perhaps no more so than in Russia, with its centuries-long traditions and its recent history.

Paskha — for which the famous Easter molded curd dish is named — is the most important day in the Russian Orthodox calendar. Housewives prepare special foods during the preceding week; a multitude of eggs is cooked, dyed, and decorated, or bought from street peddlers. Even today, eggs are dyed with the outer skins of yellow onions, the amount determining the deepness of the red that results. Wooden, porcelain, and lacquered eggs also are popular gifts.

On the eve preceding Easter Sunday, tradition calls for families to place their Kouliches (a sweet bread with raisins and nuts) and dyed eggs on long tables in the churchyard, for blessing by the priests. Even nonbelievers attend the Sunday morning service, where worshipers greet each other with the words, "Xpuctoc Bockpec! Bouctuhy Bockpec!" — "Christ Is Risen! Really Risen!" Among strangers and friends alike, a triple kiss on the cheeks is the essential Easter greeting.

Then the week of feasting and visiting begins. Koulich, the Easter bread, might center the table as the family eagerly begins with the blessed eggs, each member of the family taking one segment. Dinner progresses through cold and hot meat dishes and casseroles. The repast ends with Koulich, Paskha, and other desserts. Visits from friends for the exchange of eggs and the seasonal greeting occupy the day. *Zakuski* (snacks) might be offered: caviar on hard-boiled eggs; a variety of fruits; dark, heavy sourdough rye bread; jellied sturgeon; or salads such as Stolichnij, a potato salad which contains apples, vegetables, and cold meats, held together with mayonnaise.

Once again, Easter and spring have come to the ancient land of the Czars.

THE TRADITION OF EASTER EGGS

EASTER EGGS ARE SO MUCH A PART OF RUSSIAN HISTORY THAT THEY OFTEN REPRESENT A FAMILY'S HERITAGE. OLD PORCELAIN AND GLASS EGGS OF ALL SIZES REST ON SPECIAL STANDS IN A PLACE OF HONOR IN RUSSIAN HOMES. THROUGHOUT THE WORLD, FABERGÉ EGGS SET WITH PRECIOUS GEMS AND SEMIPRECIOUS STONES REMAIN POPULAR MUSEUM EXHIBIT ITEMS. TODAY, EGGS AS PIECES OF ART ARE BEING MADE ONCE AGAIN, MANY WITH ICONS HIDING BEHIND FABERGÉ-LIKE DOORS. WOODEN EGGS ARE HIGHLY POLISHED AND BEAR MINIATURE ORNAMENTS, CARVINGS, AND SILHOUETTES. BEJEWELED, GOLD-TRIMMED CLOISONNÉ EGGS ARE POPULAR PENDANTS.

KOULICH

(Easter Bread)

1 ounce (4 packets or equivalent) active dry yeast

1 cup (7 ounces) warm milk

4 cups flour

1 teaspoon salt

5 egg yolks, beaten

1 cup sugar

1 teaspoon vanilla (or 1 package vanillin powder)

1 cup (2 sticks) margarine

3 1/2 tablespoons oil

4 egg whites, beaten

4 cups flour

1/2 cup raisins, washed and dried

1/4 cup almonds, finely cut (or 1/2 teaspoon almond extract)

Fine bread crumbs

ICING

1 egg white

1 cup sugar

Dissolve yeast in warm milk; add 4 cups flour and stir to prevent lumps. Cover with a towel and put in a warm place until the dough doubles in size. Add salt, beaten egg yolks mixed with sugar, vanilla, margarine, and oil. Mix thoroughly, then fold in 4 beaten egg whites and additional 4 cups of flour. The pastry must not be too thick but should be well kneaded. Set aside in a warm place and when doubled in size again, add raisins and almonds, well dusted with flour for easier blending.

Place pastry in a round pan, about 8 inches in diameter and in height — perhaps a large coffee can. Cover the bottom with white parchment or waxed paper oiled on both sides; oil the sides of the pan and sprinkle with bread crumbs. Place pastry in the pan

Koulich Easter Bread made in an American coffee can waits next to the family samovar for Easter afternoon tea.

— dough should fill only 1/3 of the container; use a second, small can if necessary. Cover with a towel, and keep in a warm place. When the pastry fills the pan, bake for 55 to 60 minutes at 350° F, using the lower or middle shelf. While baking, rotate the pan carefully. When the top browns, place a wet piece of paper on top. Insert a toothpick to test: if dry, the cake is ready. Cool and ice with a mixture of egg white beaten with sugar. Koulich may be decorated with berries or chocolate.

Mrs. Natalya Visman
Moscow, Russia

PASKHA

(A Molded Curd Dish)

2 1/4 pounds fresh curds, cottage cheese, or farmer's cheese

2 tablespoons butter

4 tablespoons sour cream

Dash of salt, if needed

1/2 cup powdered sugar

1 teaspoon vanilla

1/2 cup raisins

Candied fruit peels

Mix fresh curds with butter, sour cream, salt, and powdered sugar. Process thoroughly in a blender until very smooth. Add vanilla and raisins. In Russia the paskha is kept in a special form under pressure until the day before serving, at least 24 hours. To serve, unmold and decorate the top with candied fruit peels. Eat with Koulich or as a side dish.

An acceptable substitute to the pressured pan is any container with a hole for draining the liquid, about 5″ or 6″ across and 6″ deep: a large-size frozen-topping container with a hole punched in the bottom; a clean clay-lined ceramic flower pot; or a large coffee can holed on the bottom. Line the container with waxed paper or cheesecloth, fill with paskha, and place it inside a larger bowl to catch the draining liquid. Set a plate or lid over the top, add a 2-pound weight to put pressure on the paskha, and refrigerate.

Mrs. Natalya Visman

LAMB PILAU

3 tablespoons butter
1 pound tender lamb pieces
2 onions, peeled and finely chopped
2 pomegranates, peeled
1 cup water
3 tablespoons melted butter
4 cups cooked rice

Heat butter in a saucepan and brown the meat. Add onions and brown. Remove pomegranate segments, taking care to exclude all fibrous dividing tissue. Add to the meat, cover with water, and simmer for 10 minutes or until lamb is tender. Stir melted butter into the rice and serve with the meat.

Igor Pachushkin
St. Petersburg, Russia

The variety of Easter eggs reflects centuries of tradition in Russia.

EGYPT

2nd Week of April
SHEM-EL-NESSIM
(National Holiday)

Friendship Force visitors to Cairo often are overwhelmed with the sights and sounds of this ancient culture. The land and its people are sunny, warm, and friendly. It is difficult to be blasé in the shadows of pyramids or unimpressed with the beauty of a white-sailed felucca whipping along the Nile, around which Egyptian civilizations have clustered for 4,500 years.

As all Islamic countries do, Egypt celebrates three important Muslim feasts. The "Big Feast" of Eid-el-Adha commemorates Abraham's sacrifice of his son. Earlier, the "Little Feast" of Eid-el-Saghir ends Ramadan, the holy month of fasting, with three days of rejoicing and joyous fairs. The third feast is Muled-el-Nebi, the birthday of the prophet Mohammad, who was born about 570 A.D. in Mecca.

When the ever-present sun rises on feast days, Muslims don new clothing and open the day at the mosque. Many go to the tombs of family members who died within the year and, in a long tradition, take heaping baskets of food to the poor.

Muslims and Christians alike celebrate the fourth feast, the Egyptian national holiday Shem-el-Nessim, or "Breathe the Breezes," which is observed the day after Orthodox Easter. Since the days of the pharaohs, this ancient spring festival has brought families together for a day of relaxation. Early in the morning they meet on the banks of the Nile, in a favored garden, or aboard a swift and breezy boat. Breakfast includes onions for their strong smell, salted fish, bread, and fruit.

Any feast day is an excuse for the family to eat favorite foods like dried fruits and nuts. Lamb is popular prepared in the Middle Eastern way, as kebabs. Vegetables are always in season in this sunny climate; especially favored is the eggplant casserole Musaqq'a,

a popular dish throughout the eastern Mediterranean, a result of the intermingling of cultures through the ages.

MUSAQQ'A
(Eggplant Casserole)

3 1/2 pounds (2 medium) eggplants
1 1/2 cups vegetable oil or shortening
1 large onion, chopped
2 cloves garlic, minced
1 pound ground beef
2 large tomatoes
1 small can tomato sauce
Salt and pepper to taste

Wash and peel eggplants. Cut crosswise into 1/2 inch slices and sprinkle with salt. After a few minutes, pat with a paper towel. Heat oil in a frying pan; when very hot, reduce heat and fry eggplant slices a few at a time until golden brown, turning once. Remove to a paper towel and cover with another

Konafa is a delicious Egyptian pastry of filo-like shredded dough.

paper towel to absorb excess oil. Fry onions and garlic in a little remaining oil until golden. Add and brown the meat. Drain excess fat and add 1 tomato, diced, and the tomato sauce. Stir well and simmer for 15 minutes. Add salt and pepper.

Place a layer of eggplant slices in the bottom of a 7″ x 11″ baking dish, then add a layer of meat. Make 4 or 6 layers, ending with the meat mixture. Cut the second tomato into very thin slices and arrange on top. Cover with foil and bake at 350° F for 1/2 hour, then remove foil and bake at 300° F for 10 minutes. Serves 6 to 8.

Boussaina Farid
Cairo, Egypt

KONAFA

(A Filo Dough Dessert)

1 package (16 ounces) shredded filo dough (kataifi)
12 tablespoons 3/4 butter

FILLING
1/2 cup combined nuts: walnuts, pecans, or other
1/4 cup raisins
2 teaspoons sugar
Pinch of cinnamon

SYRUP
1 cup water
1 1/2 cups sugar
2 drops each: vanilla and lemon juice

To make the syrup: Boil water and sugar to the consistency of pancake syrup; it will thicken further as it cools. Stir in flavorings and set aside to cool.

To make the cake: Melt the butter and divide into two portions. From one half, lightly cover the bottom of a 9″ or 10″ round cake pan. Tear the shredded dough into smaller pieces and place half in the dish. Drizzle the rest of the first butter evenly on top and firmly pack down. Then spread the filling and press down. Add remaining dough pieces and evenly drizzle the second half of butter, again pushing down firmly to make it compact.

Bake for 20 to 25 minutes at 350° F or until bubbly and a light golden brown. Remove from the oven and immediately pour a slow thin stream of syrup over the cake in an even criss-cross pattern. After 15 minutes, turn onto a serving plate and wait 15 more minutes before cutting into wedges. May be garnished with sweetened whipped cream and a sprinkle of nuts.

Notes: For a different filling, combine 1/2 to 3/4 cup dry ricotta cheese, 2 teaspoons sugar, and a pinch of cinnamon. Or use sweet mozzarella cheese. A Middle Eastern or international market will stock *kataifi* (long, moist strands of filo dough).

May Abdel-Wahab
Cairo, Egypt, and Miami, Florida

—AN EGYPTIAN DINING EXPERIENCE—

As family members and guests assemble in an Egyptian home, they begin with Kerkaday, a cold drink made from red hibiscus flowers. The hostess offers a main dish and a green salad tossed with oil and vinegar. Boiled white rice is served plain or laced with raisins and cinnamon. The bread is a flat round Eastern loaf of wheat or bran, similar to pita bread. For dessert, seasonal fruit is the natural choice and the meal concludes with sweetened mint tea served in small glasses.

Martha Roy
Cairo, Egypt

THAILAND

3rd Week of April
FAMILY DAY
(Wan Krop Krua)

A testament to the time-honored value of the family unit throughout Thailand's history can be seen each year during the New Year folk festival called Songkran, which culminates in Family Day on April 14. On this day Thais return once again to their family home to pay respect to their elders, to seek wisdom and counsel, to present monetary or other gifts, and to assure that tender and adequate care is provided.

Family Day includes a feast of traditional dishes, perhaps steamed chicken or fish, long noodles to symbolize many decades of life for each family member, and ever-present dips and sauces.

Even in modern society, when young people move about more often for work or education, respect for the extended family remains deeply embedded in the heart of all Thais. Traditionally the father is the head of the household, while the mother sees to the physical, spiritual, and financial nourishment of the family.

The importance placed on the family system, the oldest and smallest unit of Thai society, is reinforced each year during the festive and majestic celebration of the king's birthday on December 5, which is known as Father's Day. Likewise, August 12 is Mother's Day as Thais cherish their queen on her birthday, honoring her as the embodiment of the ideal mother.

Throughout this Constitutional Monarchy, the king's birthday is a major holiday and includes Trooping of the Colors and fireworks shimmering over the Grand Palace in Bangkok. For Buddhists, the most important festival is Visakha Puja in May, with holy days following in July. To begin their year, on the night of the first full moon, the simple but moving Majha Puja ceremony ends with candlelit processions around each temple.

Mee Grob (crispy noodles) and a bowl of Tom Yum Goong (soup) tempt Thai appetites.

NAAM PRIG PLA YAANG
(Grilled Fish Dip)

3 or 4 fresh red chilies (Prig Khee Noo)
1 dried red chili, cut and soaked
3 cloves garlic, toasted
2 shallots, toasted
1 cup fish meat, grilled and flaked
1/2 teaspoon shrimp paste, toasted
2 tablespoons lime juice
1 tablespoon fish sauce
1 teaspoon sugar

Pound the fresh and dried red chilies. Add garlic and shallots and continue pounding until well mixed into a fine paste. Combine fish meat and shrimp paste and gently add. Season with lime juice, fish sauce, and sugar. Serve with vegetables and grilled or fried fish.

Charlie Amatayakul
Bangkok, Thailand

Although fish and rice are staples of Thai cooking, soups and dips also are important. A good meal may consist of a bowl of soup and a plate heaped with fluffy rice. Sauces and dips such as Naam Prig and Naam Jim are popular with all classes of society. Fresh fruits and vegetables are plentiful and easily sold from open markets, or from floating markets on one of the KLONGS (canals) which crisscross the Bangkok cityscape.

With pungent flavors borrowed from its neighbors, China and India, Thai cuisine is spicy, sweet, sour, and salty. Garlic and other herbs hold the magic together.

TOM YUM GOONG
(Sour Shrimp Soup)

10 medium shrimp
1 cup button mushrooms (canned)
1 quart water
1 stalk lemon grass or 2 pieces lemon peel
2 magrood leaves or mint leaves, optional
1/2 teaspoon each: salt and MSG (flavor enhancer), optional
2 tablespoons fish sauce
2 tablespoons lemon or lime juice
1/2 teaspoon chili powder
8 sprigs coriander

Wash, peel, and devein shrimp; if large in size, cut into halves. Cut mushrooms to the same size. In a saucepan, boil the water and add lemon grass and magrood leaves if desired. Add the shrimp and simmer gently for 3 minutes, then add mushrooms, salt, and MSG.

Remove from heat and season with fish sauce, lemon juice, and chili powder. Spoon into individual serving dishes and garnish with sprigs of coriander. Serves 4.

Malulee Pinsuvana
Bangkok, Thailand

COCONUT PUDDING

BOTTOM LAYER
1/2 cup rice flour
1/4 cup cornstarch
1 tablespoon light brown sugar
1 cup sugar
1 cup water
2 or 3 drops red food coloring (optional)
1/2 cup water chestnuts, chopped fine

TOP LAYER
1 tablespoon rice flour
1 1/2 tablespoons cornstarch
1 1/2 cups sweet coconut milk
1 teaspoon salt
Rose petals to decorate (optional)

To make the bottom layer: Combine rice flour, cornstarch, both sugars, water, and food coloring. Mix and pour through a strainer into a saucepan. Stir over medium-low heat until well cooked. Add water chestnuts. Lower the heat, continue stirring, and cook for 5 minutes more. Remove from heat and spoon into small cups or banana-leaf cups. Set aside.

To make the top layer: Blend rice flour and corn-starch and add to the coconut milk. Add salt and stir over medium-low heat until thickened. Spoon the white mixture over the pink mixture. Cool and garnish with rose petals, if desired.

Ramyong Sakornpan
Bangkok, Thailand

Malulee Pinsuvana is the author of a popular cookbook in Bangkok.

MEE GROB
(Crispy Noodles)

1 package (8 ounces) white rice noodles
2 cups vegetable oil
1 tablespoon chopped spring onions
1/2 cup shrimp, shelled, cleaned, and cut into small pieces
2 tablespoons sliced lean pork
1 teaspoon garlic powder
2 tablespoons sugar
1 tablespoon brown bean sauce
2 tablespoons fish sauce
1 egg
1 teaspoon lemon rind, grated
1/2 cup bean sprouts
3 sprigs coriander
1 red chili, cut lengthwise

Scald rice noodles briefly in boiling water. Drain and set aside in the strainer to dry for 5 minutes, then spread noodles apart for 5 more minutes. Fry the noodles in oil until light brown. Remove and set aside.

In a wok, heat 3 tablespoons of the oil over medium heat. Stir-fry onions, shrimp, and pork, sprinkle with garlic powder, and continue for a few minutes. Add sugar, brown bean sauce, and fish sauce. Turn over a few times. Add egg and stir-fry until the egg is almost cooked. Add the fried noodles, tossing lightly until well mixed. Sprinkle the top with grated lemon rind. Serve bean sprouts beside the noodles and garnish with coriander sprigs and red chili.

Malulee Pinsuvana

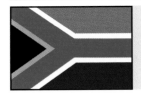

SOUTH AFRICA

4th Week of April
FREEDOM DAY
(Braai)

South Africa's stunning national flag was first raised on April 27, 1994, now celebrated with parades and pride as Freedom Day. The new constitution took effect and the first elections were held on that historic day. The flag's design seems to suggest several diverse elements of South African society coming together to form a highway green with promise for the future — a significant statement of this once-troubled nation's peaceful transition to nonracial democracy.

South Africa is a beautiful land of uncrowded vistas, sunshine, and flowers — even the deserts bloom in the spring. The republic is an intriguing union of native tribes and descendants of European settlers, each affecting the modern nation of today: the tribes offer rich, centuries-old traditions; the Dutch founded the old Atlantic port of Capetown near the southern tip; the French added their own influence; and the British eventually colonized this country of mountains and beaches, fertile farmlands, and vineyards. Freedom Day represents the joining of all these elements.

South African families celebrate with the traditional Braaivleis or Braai, an American-style barbecue which varies from an informal gathering around the open cooking fire to a formal indoor setting with large platters of barbecued meat brought sizzling to a dining table or buffet. The Braai always includes several meats: lamb chops, Boer Wars sausages similar to bratwurst, beef ribs, and perhaps chicken.

Two essential dishes complement the grilled meats: Bredie, a Dutch Afrikaan lamb and vegetable stew; and Bobotie, a Cape Malay casserole of beef or mutton with a custard top. Vegetables might be mealies (corn on the cob), creamed cauliflower, or steamed pumpkin. No Braai would be complete without Pap, made from a coarse cornmeal and served with a sauce of tomatoes, green peppers, and onions.

South Africans love rich desserts like Apple Tart with Brandy, a chocolate concoction, or perhaps Koeksisters, a plaited or cut pastry which is fried golden brown and soaked with a sugary syrup.

BOBOTIE
(A Beef Casserole)

2 onions, sliced thinly
Oil or butter
2 pounds ground beef, lamb, or mutton (or combination)
1 slice bread
1 cup milk
2 eggs
1 1/2 tablespoons sugar
2 teaspoons salt
1/2 teaspoon pepper
1 tablespoon medium curry powder
2 teaspoons turmeric
2 tablespoons vinegar or juice of 1 lemon
6 almonds, quartered
1/2 cup seedless raisins
3 tablespoons chutney (peach or regular) or apricot jam
4 lemon or bay leaves

In a heavy pan, fry onion slices lightly in oil or butter; add meat and cook slightly until crumbly. Soak bread in 1/2 cup milk; squeeze out milk and discard. Break bread into pieces. Reserve 1 egg, remaining 1/2 cup milk, and lemon leaves. Combine all other ingredients and spoon the mixture into a greased ovenproof dish. Insert rolled lemon leaves upright in the mixture.

Bake in a preheated 350° F oven 1 hour. Beat remaining egg and milk and pour over the casserole halfway through the cooking time. Serve with rice and chutney.

Janis Caccivio
Capetown, South Africa

TAMATIE BREDIE
(Lamb and Tomato Stew)

BASIC BREDIE
1 tablespoon oil
2 medium onions, chopped
2 pounds of stewing lamb, cubed
Salt and pepper to taste

THE TAMATIE VARIATION

6 tomatoes (about 2 pounds), peeled and quartered
1 green pepper, seeded and finely chopped
6 or 8 potatoes, quartered or diced
1 teaspoon sugar
1/2 teaspoon dried thyme or basil

Heat oil in a large saucepan and sauté onions until transparent. Add meat and brown quickly to seal juices. Add tomatoes, green pepper, potatoes, seasonings, sugar, and dried herbs. Simmer, covered, until vegetables are tender. If the Bredie becomes too dry, add a little water. Serve with rice. Serves 6 to 8.

Note: Bredie is a stew with as many variations as there are vegetables and seasonings. Some options are: cubed pumpkin; cabbage; potatoes, carrots, and turnips; or potatoes and water lilies with sorrel leaves, nutmeg, and lemon.

Kay Vlotman
Capetown, South Africa

A fresh strawberry sauce perfectly complements the three chocolate layers of South Africa Silk.

Jan Caccivio prepares Braai for Friendship Force guest Nancy Lawton of Colorado.

SOUTH AFRICAN SILK

1 tablespoon unflavored gelatin
1/4 cup cold water
4 egg yolks
1/2 cup sugar
1 cup milk
1/2 cup white chocolate, grated
1/2 cup milk chocolate candy, grated
1/2 cup semisweet dark chocolate, grated
1 1/2 cups whipping cream
Garnish: chocolate shavings or strawberry half

STRAWBERRY SAUCE
1 pint fresh or frozen strawberries
3 tablespoons sugar
1 tablespoon lemon juice

Dissolve gelatin in cold water. Beat egg yolks with sugar. Heat milk but do not boil. Mix a little milk with the yolk mixture, then blend in remaining milk. Stir over very low heat — to avoid curdling — until well cooked. Stir in the gelatin mixture and divide evenly into three bowls. Blend white chocolate into one, milk chocolate into the second, and dark chocolate into the third. Stir each until chocolate melts and mixtures are smooth. Put in refrigerator until cool and partially set.

Whip cream until stiff. Divide into thirds, and fold one part into each chocolate custard. Line a small round cake tin — no larger than 8 inches — with a double layer of waxed paper. Pour in the white chocolate mixture and smooth; carefully spoon in the layer of milk chocolate and gently top with dark chocolate. Refrigerate overnight.

To serve, loosen the sides and turn out onto a cake plate. Remove waxed paper and slice with a hot knife. Make a strawberry sauce by liquidizing ingredients in a blender. Ladle a pool of sauce onto each dessert plate, add a slice of silk, and garnish with chocolate shavings or a strawberry half. Serves 6 to 8.

Note: If desired, beat the raw egg whites until stiff and fold into the whipped cream before adding to each chocolate; this will result in a lighter silk.

Marlene Goddard-Hartog
Capetown, South Africa

Virginia Harder, right, says farewell to her Tzaneen hostesses on a recent Friendship Force visit.

New Zealand: Maori Hangi with Kumara Salad and Leg of Lamb

MEXICO

On May 5, 1862, the Mexican army defeated the French at the Battle of Puebla and began a celebration shared by every Mexican city and town — and almost as heartily by Norteamericano communities in the border states, where Cinco de Mayo festivals clutter May calendars. On both sides of the Rio Grande, Mexico's ancestral heritage blooms amid patriotic speeches, folk music, and special foods descended from pre-Columbian Indians and from Spanish and French conquerors.

Cinco de Mayo honors the handful of young heroes who fought valiantly in Puebla against great odds to preserve Mexican independence gained in 1810. This is a holiday usually spent informally, with relaxing hours on the beach or around the family dinner table.

Mexico is also famous for its colorful fiestas, such as one in the south in July dating from pre-Columbian times, where costumed native-born Oaxacans perform country folk dances. In December the country unites to honor the Virgin of Guadalupe with visits to the miracle site, where Mary appeared to the Indian Juan Diego in 1533.

The most stirring holiday is Independence Day, which begins just before midnight on September 15 with a reenactment of Miguel Hidalgo's call for revolution in 1810. Bells and shouts of "Viva Mexico" ring out in each state when the governor holds the flag aloft. In Mexico City, the president does the same before a great crowd in the central plaza, tolling the same bell that rang in 1810. Fireworks fill the night sky, and on the 16th, parades and speeches continue to salute the nation's history.

For this holiday, Chiles en Nogada (Chilies in Walnut Sauce) is the popular choice for a family: the green of the chilies, the white sauce, and the red pomegranate seeds echo the colors of the flag.

CHILES EN NOGADA
(Chilies in Walnut Sauce)

6 fresh California green chilies (Chiles Poblanos)
1 teaspoon oregano
1 1/2 onions, chopped
1/2 pound lean pork
2 medium tomatoes, chopped
1 whole garlic, minced
1 sprig thyme
1/2 cup almond pieces
1/4 cup raisins
50 Castilla nuts (walnuts), ground
1 cup Crema Fresca (heavy or whipping cream)
1/2 cup milk or more
Salt and black pepper to taste
Garnish: pomegranate seeds and parsley

Wash chilies, wipe dry, arrange on a broiler rack, and put in a heated broiler about 1 inch below the heat. Turn chilies often. When each is blistered and light brown, wrap them in a cotton towel and place in a plastic bag. Close bag and set aside for about 10 minutes. Peel one chili at a time, taking care not to break it open. Cut a slit lengthwise in one side of each chili, starting 1/4 inch from the stem. Carefully remove seeds, core, and white pith. Boil chilies for 5 minutes in salted water with oregano and 1/2 onion. Remove chilies and dry with a towel.

Cook pork in the water and, when tender, chop finely. Fry the remaining onion in oil, add chopped meat, and sauté for a few more minutes. Add tomato, spices, almonds, and raisins. Stirring constantly, cook for 15 minutes until the mixture is like a chunky paste. Cool and stuff the chilies.

Grind walnuts in a blender and add cream, enough milk to make a creamy sauce, and salt and pepper to taste. (For a whiter sauce, boil walnut pieces for 5 minutes in water to cover, drain and peel before grinding). To serve, arrange cooled stuffed chilies on a platter and spoon walnut sauce over the top. Garnish with pomegranate seeds and a sprig of parsley. Serves 4 to 6.

Mavi Ramirez
Tuxtla-Gutierrez, Mexico

SOPA DE PAN
(Bread Soup)

1 long, narrow French or sourdough loaf
Butter
4 small potatoes
3 small zucchini, sliced
1/2 cup green beans, cut
Cooking oil
1 large onion, thinly sliced
2 large tomatoes, thinly sliced
1 plantain, thinly sliced
4 cups chicken broth
Salt and black pepper to taste
2 teaspoons sugar
1 sprig of thyme or 1/2 teaspoon dried thyme
1 small stick cinnamon
1/2 cup raisins

Cut French bread into thin slices, lightly butter, and toast in the oven. Set aside. Peel and cut potatoes into thick slices. Boil for 5 minutes, then add zucchini and beans and continue boiling for 10 minutes. Drain and set aside. In a saucepan, lightly cook

The green, white, and red of Chiles en Nogada make this dish popular on national days. Mavi Ramirez shows the ingredients.

onions and then tomato slices in oil, setting each aside. Next fry plantain until golden, remove, and set aside. Add broth to the saucepan and stir in seasonings, sugar, and spices. Simmer for 15 minutes and remove the cinnamon stick. In a greased 9″ x 13″ casserole, layer half the bread and half of each vegetable. Sprinkle with half the raisins. Repeat a second layer, ending with plantain slices. Pour the seasoned broth over all. Bake in a preheated 350° F oven for 30 minutes. Serves 6.

Jorge Diaz Olivares
Chiapas, Mexico

CREMA DE MANGO CON NUEZ
(Mango and Pecan Cream)

5 fresh mangoes, fully ripened (soft to the touch)
Sugar to taste
2 large navel oranges, peeled, seeded, and cut into
  small pieces
1 tablespoon lemon juice
2 cups heavy whipping cream
1 cup pecan pieces
12 green and red maraschino cherries to garnish

Peel mangoes and cut into bite-size pieces, discarding pits. Add enough sugar to sweeten to your taste. Add orange pieces and lemon juice. Whip cream until stiff and fold in the pecan pieces. Fold in the fruit mixture. Serve in parfait glasses or goblets. To celebrate Cinco de Mayo, top with red and green cherries.

Linda Armendariz
Atlanta, Georgia

CARAMEL FLAN

1/3 cup sugar
6 eggs
6 tablespoons sugar
2 cups milk
1 teaspoon vanilla

Prepare a hot water bath for the flan by setting a 9″ aluminum pie pan inside a slightly larger pan. Hold down the smaller pan while you fill the larger pan with enough water to come part way up the sides of the smaller pan. Remove this pan and warm the larger pan of water in a preheated 350° F oven.

Over low heat, melt 1/3 cup sugar in the smaller pan, shaking and tilting to coat the sides. When the sugar is caramelized but not hard, set aside and keep warm. In a blender, beat together the eggs, 6 tablespoons sugar, milk, and vanilla. Pour into the caramelized pan and return it to the larger pan of water. Bake at 350° F for about 25 minutes. Test the custard by gently pushing in the center with the back of a spoon. If done, a crevice should form.

Remove the custard pan and chill at once. When cold, loosen the hardened caramel around the sides with the tip of a knife. Place a large serving plate on top and invert quickly — to allow the flan to slip free. To serve, cut into wedges and spoon juices on top.

Linda Armendariz

Father Jorge Diaz Olivares smiles his approval of a Mexican sombrero for Cinco de Mayo.

New Zealand

2nd Week of May
MOTHER'S DAY

Mother's Day in New Zealand, the Land of the Long White Cloud, starts with the children serving Mother her breakfast in bed, under supervision of Dad, beginning with freshly squeezed orange or grapefruit juice from trees in the garden. For young children, toast spread with peanut butter and homemade marmalade suffices; older children manage dishes a little more elaborate. When children are grown, Dad takes over.

After a family service at church, mothers receive a long-stemmed white flower, perhaps a chrysanthemum. Then the family gathers for an elaborate luncheon, or a simple informal one, to honor each mother in the extended family. As in the United States, Mother's Day — or Te Ra Mo Nga Whaea in the native Maori tongue — is the second Sunday in May.

The menu for this special luncheon might feature a roast of lamb, beef, or chicken — or the less formal Bacon and Egg Pie. Pumpkin soup is a favorite starter, with a salad of kumara, the New Zealand sweet potato which was the most important cultivated food of the Maori people and important to their religious observances.

Dessert would always — always — be Pavlova, a meringue decorated with whipped cream and fruit named for the Russian ballerina and known by many as New Zealand's national dessert. Devoted fans argue about which of two baking methods is best.

Mother's Day may have grown out of Mothering Sunday, observed by English churches since the 17th century—even adult children "out in service" to a wealthy family would return home with small gifts to "go a-mothering." Other countries in Europe followed the English tradition, and in the United States in 1872, Julia Ward Howe suggested a Mother's Day

dedicated to peace. In 1908 Anna Jarvis Grafton of West Virginia honored her mother by wearing a carnation on the second Sunday of May, and this gesture grew to become an official American observance in 1915, now shared by New Zealand.

Leg of Lamb with Stuffing is the perfect entrée for Mother's Day.

LEG OF LAMB WITH STUFFING

Leg of lamb, deboned by butcher
3 cups soft bread crumbs
1 can (14 ounces) crushed pineapple, drained
1 apple, cored, peeled, and grated
1/4 cup fresh mint, chopped
1 teaspoon each: fresh chopped ginger and garlic
2 eggs
Salt and pepper to taste

Prepare the stuffing by mixing together all ingredients except lamb. Open the deboned leg of lamb, spread out the stuffing, and roll, reforming the leg and tying with string at intervals. Place in a baking pan, cover, and cook in a moderate oven at 325° F until the juices run clear, at least 20 minutes per pound or until a meat thermometer registers 145° to 150° F. Refrigerate before slicing and serve cold. Cook surplus stuffing in a flat oven dish, and cut into cubes to serve on a platter with the meat. Serves 6 to 8.

Marion Ruscoe
Wanganui, New Zealand

Val Main decorates her version of Pavlova.

CURRIED PEACH SALAD

2 to 4 onions, sliced in rings
1 teaspoon salt
2 teaspoons each: turmeric and curry powder
Scant 1/2 cup wine vinegar
1 large can (29 ounces) sliced peaches
1/2 cup sugar, or to taste
1 1/2 tablespoons cornflour (cornstarch) mixed with
*   water*

In a saucepan, simmer onion rings, salt, turmeric, curry, and vinegar until onions are soft. Add peaches, juice, and sugar, and cook until sugar is dissolved. Stir in the cornstarch mixture and heat until thickened. Cool. Serve cold with meat and salads. Keeps for a long period in the refrigerator. Serves 6 to 8.

Shirley Andrews
Carterton, New Zealand

PAVLOVA (1)

Whites of 4 large eggs
Pinch of cream of tartar
1/2 cup plus 1 tablespoon castor (fine) sugar
1 teaspoon vanilla
2 teaspoons malt vinegar
1 tablespoon cold water
2 teaspoons cornstarch
1/2 cup plus 1 tablespoon castor (fine) sugar
Whipped cream
Strawberries, kiwi, or passion fruit
Chocolate chips (optional)

Beat egg whites with a good pinch of cream of tartar, until stiff. Add 1/2 cup plus 1 tablespoon sugar and beat well. Then beat in the remaining ingredients and, lastly, fold in the remaining sugar but do not beat.

Shape into a round mound on the shiny side of foil placed on an oven tray. Bake in the center of the oven at 300° to 325° F for approximately 1 1/2 hours. Turn out immediately onto a large flat plate and carefully peel off the foil. When cool, decorate with whipped cream and top with strawberries, kiwi, or passion fruit. A sprinkling of chocolate chips is optional. After decorating, Pavlova may be refrigerated for 2 to 3 hours before serving.

Val Main
Wanganui, New Zealand

PAVLOVA (2)

3 egg whites
3 tablespoons cold water
1/4 teaspoon salt
1 cup castor (fine) sugar
1 teaspoon vinegar
1/2 teaspoon vanilla
3 heaping teaspoons cornstarch
Whipped cream
Strawberries, kiwi, or passion fruit

Beat egg whites until stiff and continue beating steadily at medium speed while adding ingredients. First add water and salt, then gradually add sugar. Beat for about 5 minutes, then add vinegar and vanilla. Fold in the cornstarch. Pile in a round shape onto a sheet of greased paper on an oven tray or cookie sheet. Bake at 250° F for 1 hour. Turn off the oven and do not remove until the oven is cold. Top with whipped cream and decorate with strawberries, kiwi, or passion fruit.

Noreen McLachlan
Hamilton, New Zealand

Colorful Kumara Salad is made from New Zealand sweet potatoes, a favorite of the Maori people.

KUMARA SALAD

2 pounds or more kumara (sweet potatoes), cooked,
*   peeled, and cubed*
1 red onion, chopped
1/2 red pepper, diced
1/2 green pepper, diced
1 can (11 ounces) mandarin oranges, drained
1 can (14 ounces) pineapple pieces, drained
Curry powder to taste
Salad dressing of choice
Cheddar cheese, grated (optional)

Prepare and combine all ingredients with the dressing: a mixture of Thousand Island dressing and mayonnaise, or a light potato salad dressing, is suggested. If desired, add a small amount of grated Cheddar cheese just prior to serving. An ideal Mother's Day dish, Kumara Salad can be made 2 or 3 days in advance. Serves 6 to 8.

Marion Ruscoe
Wanganui, New Zealand

NORWAY

3rd Week of May
CONSTITUTION DAY

Norwegians are joyful in celebration of their constitution, which was signed on May 17, 1814: the country erupts with parades in every city and village. This happy spring festival is important in a country whose winters are long and hard. But above all, it's an exciting time for children as they gather in the town square to watch the flag-raising, then form into parades behind banners and school bands. In Oslo thousands of children march past the Royal Palace for a glimpse of King Harald and Queen Sonja. Later, family picnics might include sports and competitions for the children.

Many adults and children wear colorful *bunads*, the distinctive folk costumes which have helped to uphold Norway's traditions and regional identity. The reds and blues of the flag, along with blacks and greens, are accented by white blouses. Embroidered bodices, gold and silver ornamentation, and tassels abound. In a 1994 Bergen festival, 120 different *bunads* were worn, each identifying a community or valley.

Families in this land of glaciers, fjords, and the midnight sun love to celebrate with festivals, midsummer bonfires, and special days for St. Olav and explorer Leif Ericson. They jubilantly commemorate May 8, 1945, when five years of occupation ended and the constitutional monarchy had survived yet again.

Here, seafood and fish are rushed to table from lake, stream, or ocean; salmon, cod, mackerel, and herring are prepared in every imaginable way. Reindeer steaks, lutefisk, thin *flatbrod*, and Geitost (a brown goat cheese) are typically Norse. Strawberries, cloudberries, lingonberries, and arctic bramble berries are summer favorites.

Wearing her bunad, *Norway's distinctive folk costume, Miriam Henriksen presents a tray of Norwegian* smorbrod.

THE KOLDTBORD AND THE SMORBROD

Norwegians take great pride in presenting food in an attractive way. Their version of Sweden's famous *smörgäsbord*, called *koldtbord*, must be attractively presented. Colorful table runners and mats often replace tablecloths, always accented with flowers, from a single rose to a bowl of freshly cut blooms.

As in most Scandinavian countries, a popular food is the open-faced sandwich called *smorbrod*. One's own imagination and devotion to design can take a *smorbrod* in any direction; the secret is making them look as good as they taste.

The open sandwich is served at a well-set table and eaten with knives and forks. A diner often begins with a fish sandwich perhaps with lightly smoked sardines, shrimp, or marinated salmon called *gravlaks*. Then comes *smorbrod* with meat — paper-thin slices of roast beef, pork, or boiled ham which are rolled, twisted, or folded, with bacon as a second meat choice. Other proteins are egg and Swiss, Cheddar, Jarlsberg, Havarti, or Geitost cheese. The top layer of a *smorbrod*, the garnish, is important to its look and taste and can include colorful vegetable slices, twists and strips, and sprinkles of minced herbs, greens, and olives.

To make mustard sauce: Mix first 6 ingredients, then add oil a little at a time while stirring. Refrigerate until used.

To make *smorbrods*: Remove salmon from the marinade. Cut into thin slices. Layer pieces of crusty white or multigrain bread with butter, a lettuce leaf, and salmon slices. Top with mustard sauce, serving extra sauce in a side bowl.

Miriam Henriksen
Oslo, Norway

MARINATED SALMON AND MUSTARD SMORBROD

2 to 3 tablespoons whole white pepper, ground
1/3 cup salt
1/3 cup sugar
2 bunches fresh dill
2 1/4 pounds salmon, frozen

MUSTARD SAUCE
2 to 3 tablespoons prepared yellow mustard
1 tablespoon sugar
1/2 to 1 tablespoon vinegar
1/4 teaspoon salt
1/8 teaspoon white pepper
2 or 3 tablespoons fresh dill
3 tablespoons oil

Several days in advance, marinate salmon: Mix first 4 ingredients and place 1/3 of the mixture in a glass dish. Partially defrost the salmon and split into 2 fillets. Do not remove skin. Place one fillet skin side down in the dish, then add 1/3 more marinade, the other fillet, and the remaining marinade. Cover with foil or plastic wrap and refrigerate for 2 or 3 days, turning fish twice each day.

REKESMORBROD

1/2 cup mayonnaise
1/2 cup whipped cream
6 slices crusty white bread, buttered
6 lettuce leaves
3 hard-boiled eggs, sliced
1 pound small shrimp, boiled and peeled
Lemon slices

Mix mayonnaise with whipped cream. On each bread slice, place a lettuce leaf, then a row of egg slices. Mound shrimp on each sandwich and top with 2 tablespoons mayonnaise mixture. Decorate with a lemon slice. Serve with additional lemon slices for sprinkling more juice over the sandwich if desired. Makes 6.

VARIATIONS ON THE SMORBROD

EGGERORE AND SMOKED SALMON

Lightly beat 6 eggs, 6 tablespoons water, milk, or cream, and 1 teaspoon salt. Put 1 1/2 tablespoons butter in a saucepan, add the egg mixture, and stir over low heat, lifting with a fork to allow mixture on top to flow to the bottom. Occasionally move the fork through the eggs until they have stiffened. Cover a white or multigrain bread slice with egg mixture, top with large slices of smoked salmon, and garnish with a little fresh dill.

JARLSBERG CHEESE

Thinly slice Jarlsberg or any yellow cheese with a wire cheese cutter and place overlapping slices on a bread slice of choice. Top with chopped red pepper or slices of grapes or oranges.

LIVERWURST AND MUSHROOM

Line rye bread with thin liverwurst slices, add mushroom slices browned in butter, and decorate with a line of mayonnaise and bacon crumbles.

ROAST BEEF WITH RÉMOULADE SAUCE

Mix 1 cup mayonnaise, 1/2 cup whipped cream, 1 tablespoon capers, 2 or 3 tablespoons chopped pickles, and 1 or 2 tablespoons chopped parsley. Mix well and add vinegar and sugar to taste. Spread slices of bread with Rémoulade Sauce and arrange slices of roast beef and raw onions on top.

BLOTKAKE

4 eggs

3/4 cup sugar

1 scant cup flour

1 teaspoon baking powder

3 to 4 tablespoons liquid: milk, juice, lemonade, white wine, sherry, or liqueur

1 pint whipping cream

1/3 cup sugar

4 cups fresh berries: strawberries, raspberries, or cloudberries

Butter the bottom of a 9-inch springform pan. Beat eggs and sugar until the mixture is stiff. Combine flour and baking powder and fold gently into the eggs, until the batter becomes smooth. Place into the pan and bake for 25 minutes on the lower shelf of a preheated oven at 350°–375° F. Set aside for a few minutes, then remove cake to cool on a wire rack.

Split the cake into two layers and dribble half of the chosen liquid over each cake half, especially around the edges, but do not allow it to get soggy. Whip cream and add 1 teaspoon sugar. Set aside 1 cup of berries, cut the rest into small pieces, and add remaining sugar. Spread berry pieces on the bottom layer, add 1/3 of the whipped cream, top with the second layer, and cover the entire cake with the remaining whipped cream. Decorate the top with the whole berries. Serves 8. *Velbekomme!* Enjoy!

Miriam Henriksen
Oslo, Norway

Three popular smorbrod: *salmon and scrambled egg, ham with asparagus and radishes, and shrimp with sliced, boiled eggs.*

PACIFIC SHORES, U.S.A.

4th Week of May
FRIENDSHIP FORCE RECEPTION

The sunny Pacific shores of California and Hawaii have attracted adventurers since well before the United States declared independence from England. Beautiful weather, excellent farmland, and the warmth of both coastlines — between them more than 2,000 miles of sand and surf — brought waves of immigrants to this land of opportunity.

Spanish explorers first discovered the pleasures of California, which became a state in 1850 soon after gold was discovered. Other lures were its fertile valleys fed by Sierra Nevada snows, railroads that conquered the western mountains, and the 1862 discovery by a Hungarian newcomer that grapes would grow in the lush valleys. Oil in 1921, the dust bowls of the 1930s, and World War II brought more seekers of fortune and sunshine.

Hawaii's history goes back a thousand years, to the first arrival of Polynesians by sailing canoe. Captain Cook's reports in 1778 began an influx of Europeans, Asians, and American mainlanders from back east. Hawaii happily became the 50th American state on August 21, 1959, now celebrated as Admission Day.

California and Hawaii: exciting, golden lands of sunshine and a grand cultural mix that fills the air with the twang of ukelele and steel guitar, Cinco de Mayo festivities, hibiscus and towering redwoods, Rose Bowl and Chinese New Year parades, and jazz, jumping frog, and wine festivals.

Mild climates delight Friendship Force visitors at welcoming receptions which showcase the bounty of both states — especially if the fruit is California- or Hawaii-grown, the cheese comes from state dairy farms, and the wine is white Zinfandel or California Chablis. Soft Hawaiian melodies or lively mariachi music and floating candles on the backyard pool add to the warmth of the welcome.

Visitors are intrigued by California cuisine, the latest trend-setting innovation which takes fresh ingredients from fields, farms, and coastal waters and blends them with the latest frontier spirit: expert cooking techniques, creativity, verve, and the belief that one has discovered a new art form.

Dorothy Iverson shows her granddaughters how to serve Jalapeño Jam.

SMOKED SALMON BUTTER

8 ounces cream cheese
3 tablespoons mayonnaise
3 tablespoons onion, finely chopped
2 teaspoons horseradish
1 tablespoon lemon juice, fresh or bottled
1/4 teaspoon liquid smoke
1 1/2 cups canned red salmon

Smoked Salmon Butter adds to a colorful reception table.

Soften cream cheese and add mayonnaise, onion, horseradish, lemon juice, and liquid smoke. Drain salmon well, flake, and add. Mix and refrigerate; chilling for several hours improves the flavor. Mound onto a serving plate and surround with saltines, wheat crackers, or chips. Provide a pâté knife.

Leta Wright
Honolulu, Hawaii

CHEESE PUFFS WITH OLIVES

2 cups sharp Cheddar cheese, grated
1/2 cup butter, softened
1 cup all-purpose flour, sifted
1 teaspoon paprika
1/2 teaspoon salt (optional)
48 stuffed green olives

Blend cheese with butter; stir in flour, paprika and salt, if desired. Mix well. Wrap 1 teaspoon of mixture around each olive, covering completely. Arrange on a baking sheet and freeze firm. When frozen, remove

and place in a plastic bag; fasten tightly and return to the freezer. When ready to serve, return to a baking sheet and bake for 15 minutes at 400° F. Cheese Puffs are best served hot. Serves 10–15.

Kay Lanz
Spring Valley, California

POLENTA/PESTO/TOMATO APPETIZERS

3 cups water
1 teaspoon Italian seasoning
2 tablespoons butter
Salt to taste
1 cup polenta (cornmeal)
Pesto
1 jar marinated sun-dried tomatoes
Feta cheese, crumbled
Pine nuts (optional)

Bring water to a boil and add Italian seasoning, butter, and salt. Gradually whisk in the polenta and whisk for 5 minutes. Place in the top of a double boiler over boiling water and cook for 15 to 20 minutes. Spread evenly in a jelly-roll pan approximately 10″ x 12″ — the polenta layer should be from 1/3- to 1/2-inch thick. Refrigerate overnight. Reward yourself with a glass of California wine!

Next day, spread the polenta with enough pesto to cover well. Take tomatoes from the jar and remove extra olive oil by pressing between paper towels. Remove some or all tomato seeds and cut tomatoes into 1/4-inch julienne strips. Place on top of the pesto. Sprinkle with feta cheese crumbles and, if desired, pine nuts. To facilitate cutting into 2-inch squares, score or cut the polenta layer before adding pesto.

Joyce Caulfield
Larkspur, California

The fruits of California and Hawaii show their best on a Fruit Pizza.

JALAPEÑO JAM

6 to 8 jalapeño peppers, to taste
6 green bell peppers
10 cups sugar
2 1/4 cups vinegar
2 packs liquid pectin
Green food coloring (optional)

Wearing rubber gloves to protect hands, remove seeds from jalapeño peppers and place peppers in a blender with green peppers. When blended, add to a large kettle in which sugar and vinegar has been mixed. Boil for 1 full minute, add liquid pectin and food coloring, if desired, and continue to boil for another minute. Pour into 14 to 16 jam jars to cool and set to jelly thickness. (Two-part lids and paraffin are not needed.) Serve over cream cheese, with your favorite crackers.

Dorothy Iverson
Santa Barbara, California

FRUIT PIZZA

1 package sugar cookie dough or pastry of your choice

8 ounces cream cheese, softened

1/4 cup sugar

1 teaspoon vanilla

Fresh fruit: bananas, apples, peaches, pineapple, melon, strawberries, and kiwi

GLAZE

3/8 cup water

1/8 cup fresh lemon juice

1/4 cup fresh orange juice

1/4 cup sugar

1 tablespoon cornstarch

Dash of salt

Roll out sugar cookie dough and place on a greased, floured round pizza pan, using flour on the hands as well. Bake according to directions. Mix cream cheese, sugar, and vanilla and spread on the cooled crust. Cut fruits and arrange on top. For glaze, mix all ingredients and boil for 1 minute. Cool and pour over the fruit. Refrigerate.

Betty Rose
Knoxville, Tennessee

SAVORY FIGS

18 California dried figs

36 water chestnuts (12-ounce can)

18 slices thin ham, cut into long strips

3/4 cup soy sauce

3 ounces sherry

1 1/2 tablespoons sugar

1 1/2 cloves garlic, pressed

3/4 teaspoon ground ginger

Snip and discard fig stems. Cut figs in half and press a water chestnut onto each half. Wrap in ham strips and secure with toothpicks. Place in a shallow dish.

Combine soy sauce, sherry, sugar, garlic, and ginger. Mix thoroughly and pour over the figs. Marinate for 2 hours, turning once or twice. Drain and arrange on a serving platter.

Note: For a hot hors d'oeuvre, wrap the figs in bacon, halved lengthwise, and broil until bacon is crisp, about 8 minutes, turning to brown on both sides.

Melenie Dickinson
Belmont, California

CAFÉ AU LAIT SQUARES

4 packages unflavored gelatin

3 cups hot water

3 tablespoons instant coffee

1 tablespoon sugar

1 can sweetened condensed milk

Frozen whipped cream

Grated chocolate

Mix gelatin and water with a wire whisk. Add coffee, sugar, and milk. Refrigerate until set. For a reception table, cut into small squares or rectangles, place each in the smallest size muffin-tin liner, add a dollop of whipped cream, and top with grated chocolate. As dessert, cut into larger squares and increase the amount of garnish.

Leta Wright

GULF STATES, U.S.A.

5th Week of May
DINNER ON THE GROUNDS

Driving through the southern states bordering the Gulf of Mexico, one will find steepled country churches with neatly kept cemeteries and long rows of wooden tables waiting under shade trees. In late May or other warm month, one might happen on a unique church event that had its beginnings in 1866 in Mississippi with the first decoration of Confederate graves.

Through the years the uniquely southern Decoration Day expanded into an all-day event with a morning sermon followed by the cleaning of church property, decoration of graves, a song session, and a spread of finger food laid out on white paper under the trees — commonly known as "dinner on the grounds." In time, permanent tables sprouted beneath the trees as the event evolved yet again into Reunion Day, Homecoming, or Church Fair Sunday.

Family reunions in a park or church grove take the same form in the South: someone organizes activities to keep the children busy; everyone else brings time-tested casseroles and one chicken, fried or baked in a pie. The dessert table groans and sways from cakes, pies, puddings, and fresh-churned ice cream. White paper still covers the tables, along with oilcloth and old quilts, and wildflowers in canning jars vie with more decorous blossoms from home gardens.

The early song sessions were so popular that a new tradition was added to dinner on the grounds — all-day singings. In the summer, two-week singing schools, using the Rudiment songbook and no musical instruments, taught new generations. Some chose shaped-note or "fa-sol-la" singing, where notes are written as squares, triangles, dia-monds, or circles. There are also Christian harmony, with seven shapes, and round-note songbooks. Sacred Harp singings, named for the 1844 songbook, still occur throughout the South, often lasting two days.

For earlier generations who worked in the fields, Sunday singings were a social occasion that sent them back to the fields with a lighter heart. So do church and family reunions today if they include singing, fried chicken, and fixin's for dinner on the grounds.

—THE HISTORY OF DECORATION DAY—

On April 26, 1866, Civil War widows in Columbus, Mississippi, performed an act of generosity which evolved into today's Memorial Day. By chance, one day later a similar group in Columbus, Georgia, decorated their own Confederate graves, and again by chance the graves of Union solders in Carbondale, Illinois, were decorated on April 29 following a speech by General John A. Logan. Two years later the general decreed that a national Memorial Day should be held each May 30 — a date chosen, it is believed, because more flowers would be in bloom. Although Confederate Memorial Day remained April 26 through many generations, the national day of remembrance has always been the last Monday in May. What makes the decoration of graves by the Mississippi women special is that they were the first to honor the war dead — and the only ones in that long-ago April to decorate enemy graves as well as their own. It happened in a burial ground known as Friendship Cemetery.

Alice Josephson of Cocoa Beach, Florida, checks on the food laid out for dinner on the grounds.

CRISPY OVEN-FRIED SOUTHERN CHICKEN

1 cup dry bread or cracker crumbs

1/2 cup Parmesan cheese, grated

1/2 teaspoon each: paprika and garlic salt

1/4 teaspoon black pepper

2 tablespoons parsley, chopped

8 tablespoons (1/2 cup) margarine

3-pound chicken, cut up, or 8 pieces of choice

Combine crumbs, cheese, paprika, garlic salt, pepper, and parsley. Melt margarine. Dip chicken pieces into margarine and roll in the crumb mixture. Place on a lightly greased baking pan, being careful not to let the chicken pieces touch. Bake for about 1 hour at 350° F, until meat is no longer pink; do not turn the chicken. Let cool. Wrap loosely in foil until ready to eat. Serves 8.

Joyce Allred
Trussville, Alabama

FROZEN PEA SALAD

1/3 medium head lettuce, torn into pieces

1 small package frozen green peas, cooked and cooled

1 medium onion, chopped

2 stalks celery, chopped

1 cup mayonnaise

1 tablespoon sugar

Salt and pepper to taste

1/2 cup grated Cheddar cheese

4 to 6 bacon strips, crisp and crumbled

Wash and dry enough lettuce for 6 servings and arrange in a glass bowl. Spread peas, onion, and celery on top. Cover with mayonnaise mixed with sugar, salt, and pepper. Sprinkle with cheese and bacon. Cover with plastic wrap and refrigerate for 6 hours before serving. Serves 6.

Helen Shepard
Dunedin, Florida

Joyce Allred of Alabama sets out her crispy oven-fried southern chicken.

BAKED PINEAPPLE

*2 cans (20 ounces) pineapple tidbits in unsweetened
    juice*
1/2 cup self-rising flour
1/2 cup sugar
2 cups grated cheese (mild or medium Cheddar)
1 roll Ritz or butter crackers, crushed
8 tablespoons (1/2 cup) butter or margarine

Place pineapple in a 9″ x 13″ baking dish. Mix flour and sugar; sprinkle over the pineapple. Top with cheese, then enough crushed crackers to cover, and dot with the butter. Bake in the oven at 325° F for 40–45 minutes, until bubbling. Serves 12.

Elsie Dudley
Montgomery, Alabama

CREOLE BREAD PUDDING

*3 cups stale French bread, with crusts, torn into small
    pieces*
1/2 cup raisins
3 tablespoons butter
2 cups milk
3/4 cup sugar
2 eggs, beaten
1 teaspoon vanilla

Butter a 1-quart round casserole dish; add bread pieces and sprinkle raisins on top. In a saucepan, over low heat, melt butter and add milk and sugar. Beat eggs in a small bowl, mix in a few tablespoons of the milk mixture, then add the egg mixture to the saucepan. When well heated, remove from the stove and add vanilla. Pour over the bread and raisins.

Bake for 30 minutes in a preheated 350° F oven. Remove and allow to rest for 30 minutes before serving warm with the sauce.

To make the sauce: With a wire whisk, beat 4 large egg yolks and 2/3 cup sugar in the top of a double boiler until light and fluffy. Gradually stir in 1 cup white wine and cook over very hot water until thick, stirring constantly. Blend in 1 tablespoon rum or kirsch. Makes about 1 2/3 cups. For an outdoor meal, keep the sauce warm in a thermos.

Geraldine Beaird
Baton Rouge, Louisiana

ANN'S MACARONI AND CHEESE

16 ounces small elbow macaroni, cooked
6 tablespoons margarine or butter
8 tablespoons flour
5 cups milk
6 cups Cheddar cheese, grated, divided

Cook macaroni and set aside. In a saucepan, make a white sauce by melting margarine, blending in flour, then adding milk a little at a time. Stir until it thickens and 5 1/2 cups of grated cheese. Mix in the macaroni and pour into a greased 9″ x 13″ pan. Sprinkle with the remaining cheese and bake at 350°F for 30 to 40 minutes. Serve hot. Serves 12.

Jean Butterworth
Birmingham, Alabama

Brazil: Freijoada

CHINA (TAIWAN)

1st Week of June
DRAGON BOAT FESTIVAL

For Taiwanese, three things come to mind when the Dragon Boat Festival is mentioned: sweet-smelling Tsungtzu, the most traditional food; lively boat races; and beautiful fragrant pouches made of spices and sandalwood powder and given to children as necklaces. Occurring on the 5th day of the 5th moon, the special day comes in early June on the western calendar and is one of the three most important Chinese holidays.

The festival commemorates the drowning suicide of Chu Juan, an ancient patriot and revered poet, in despair over his country's future. Legend states that boats were launched to try to find his body and rice dumplings were thrown into the river — some say to feed the sea creatures and keep them away from Chu Juan.

Today two legacies from the poet's death are the favorite food Tsungtzu, filled dumplings of glutinous rice wrapped in bamboo leaves, and the races with boats whose bows are carved dragon heads.

Also known as Poet's Day, this occasion is a family day for picnicing or dining at home, attending the boat races, holding reunions, and listening to poetry recitals.

The aromatic pouch necklaces prepared for children are intended to drive evil spirits away, as in earlier days they warded off insects and germs. Adults are protected against evil spirits with a small drink of realgar wine, a mixture of a Chinese medicine and rice wine.

With the popular Tsungtzu, the family will eat vegetables or soup and perhaps bean soy mixed with peanut powder. A welcome dessert in hot summer months is icy Almond Bean Curd.

Jau-Hsien Huang holds the Tsungtzu dumplings which are traditional for the Dragon Boat Festival.

TSUNGTZU

(Dumplings with Rice and Pork)

12 dried bamboo leaves

2 1/2 cups (16 ounces) long-grain glutinous rice

7 ounces uncured bacon or pork roast

2 tablespoons dried small shrimp

6 dried mushrooms

Vegetable oil

4 tablespoons soy sauce

1 teaspoon sugar

1/2 teaspoon sesame oil

1/4 teaspoon salt

Dash of pepper

4 tablespoons fried shallot flakes or pieces of shallot root

30 to 40 raw peanut pieces

6 lengths cotton string

Soak bamboo leaves to soften; then scald briefly in hot water. Drain and set aside. Rinse rice until the water runs clear, soak for 4 hours and drain. Place cheesecloth in the bottom of a steamer basket, add rice, and flatten, splashing with small amount of water. Steam rice for 30 minutes until soft.

Cut pork into large cubes. Rinse shrimp. Soak mushrooms, remove stems, and slice. In a saucepan with 4 tablespoons or more vegetable oil, fry shrimp, meat, and mushrooms until fragrant. Add soy sauce, sugar, sesame oil, salt, and pepper; cover the pan and simmer a few minutes. Remove from the pan, add half the shallots, and divide the mixture into 6 piles, retaining the sauce. Mix rice, sauce, and remaining shallots and again divide into 6 portions. Boil peanuts until soft and divide into 6 more piles.

To assemble: Overlap 2 bamboo leaves and fold into a conical shape. Into the bamboo cone in layers, place half of 1 pile of rice mixture, then 1 entire pile of shrimp and meat, then 1 full pile of peanuts. Cover with the remaining rice from 1 pile. Fold leaves over and around to form a Tsungtzu and tie tightly with string. After completing 6 Tsungtzu, place in the steamer and steam over high heat for 25 minutes.

Dr. Jau-Hsien Huang
Taipei, Taiwan

ALMOND BEAN CURD

1/3 rounded cup (2 ounces) short grain rice

8 cups water

1 cup sugar

6 cups water

3/4 ounce agar-agar (gelatinous dried seaweed)

4 tablespoons almond extract

1 can (16 ounces) fruit cocktail, undrained

Rinse rice, soak in water for 1 hour, and drain. Add 3/4 cup water and purée in a blender. Dissolve sugar

Tsungtzu are wrapped in bamboo leaves.

in 8 cups water and add. In a saucepan, bring 6 additional cups water to a boil, add washed agar-agar, and boil until it dissolves. Add rice purée, stirring constantly until it boils again. Remove from heat and add almond extract. Sieve the mixture, pour into a mold, and cool. Chill in refrigerator for 20 minutes.

When set, cut the almond bean curd into bite-size pieces and combine with fruit cocktail and ice cubes in a serving bowl. If unsweetened fruit cocktail is used, sweeten the juice with 2/3 cup sugar.

Donna Lin
Taipei, Taiwan

Because fragrant pouches, called hsiang pao, *are stitched and embroidered by hand, they convey a feeling of warmth toward those who receive them. The gaily decorated pouches are hung from colorful cords. Since it is believed that new brides bring good luck, at the first Dragon Boat Festival after her wedding a bride might make as many as 200 pouches for relatives, friends, and neighborhood children.*

A CHINESE BREAKFAST AND DINNER

BREAKFAST IS IMPORTANT TO THE INDUSTRIOUS PEOPLE OF THE REPUBLIC OF CHINA. SOYBEAN MILK IS SERVED COLD OR HOT, EITHER SWEET OR SALTY. CONGEE, COOKED LIKE GRITS, IS TOPPED WITH HOT SPICY CITRON CUCUMBERS, SALTED FRIED PEANUTS, MARINATED CABBAGES, OR SALTY DUCK EGGS. RECTANGULAR SESAME SEED CAKES ARE FOLDED AND STUFFED WITH LONG DOUGHNUTS.

CHINESE FAMILIES MAY EAT A LIGHT LUNCH OR A HEAVIER MEAL — SEVERAL DISHES OF CHICKEN, DUCK, FISH, MEAT, OR SEAFOOD; SOUP AND VEGETABLES; AND, ON EVERY OCCASION, RICE. LARGE BOWLS AND PLATTERS ARE CLUSTERED ON A ROUND TABLE, SO THAT EVERYONE CAN REACH EVERY DISH. IF A DESSERT IS SERVED, IT MIGHT BE FRUIT OR SWEET SOUP. OOLONG OR HOT JASMINE TEA COMPLETES THE MEAL.

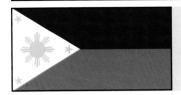

PHILIPPINES

2nd Week of June
INDEPENDENCE DAY

For freedom-loving Filipinos, Independence Day on June 12 celebrates self-government, which came to the islands in 1898 after centuries of foreign domination. A national holiday free from work, it is the day for a family picnic in Luneta Park watching the gigantic parade along with the president of the republic, the cabinet, the diplomatic corps, and war veterans. Or it might mean an informal gathering at an improvised table in the front yard.

If family and friends gather at home in the sala before a more sumptuous meal, the traditional centerpiece on the dining table might be a roast pig in fresh banana leaves, to be served with a spicy liver sauce. Inside or out, the group eats most foods by hand, standing, catching up on family news, and sharing glasses of local beer or fresh-squeezed juices laced with rum or gin.

Family ties are important to Filipinos, who love an excuse to celebrate holy days, feast days of barrio patron saints, popular local festivals, and Philippine-American Friendship Day on July 4, formerly Independence Day.

The centuries-long influence of the Spanish, Chinese, Malays, and Americans shows in the variety of foods in the islands. Adobo is a stew prepared with chicken, pork, or both meats — considered to be the Filipino national dish. A perfect do-ahead dish that travels well, Adobo is usual for the Independence Day picnic or festive family lunch.

The dessert would be Ginumiz; its red and blue gelatin cubes, white blanket of coconut cream, and decorative paper flags add to the patriotic fervor on Independence Day.

For most Filipinos, the national fish is Bangus. For festive occasions the milkfish is deboned and cut up, then cooked with pork, onions, vegetables such as peas and diced potatoes, and raisins. Replaced inside the marinated fish shell, it is tied with string and browned in oil. As with other Asian countries, rice is a staple with the meat course or in desserts.

CHICKEN AND PORK ADOBO

2 pounds pork (2-inch pork spareribs or cubed pork)
2 pounds chicken, cut into serving pieces
1 cup water
1/2 cup vinegar
1 teaspoon salt
1/4 cup soy sauce
3 to 4 cloves garlic, mashed
1/4 teaspoon peppercorns, crushed
1 or 2 bay leaves
2 tablespoons cooking oil
White rice, cooked

Remove as much fat as possible from the pork ribs. Stew chicken and pork pieces for about 10 minutes in a mixture of water, vinegar, salt, soy sauce, mashed garlic, peppercorns, and bay leaf. When the meat is tender, drain liquid, and set aside. Brown the meat and chopped garlic in hot cooking oil. Return the liquid and cook over moderate heat for another 10 minutes until the sauce has thickened. If needed, thicken with cornstarch mixed with water. Serve over white rice. Serves 6 to 8.

Helena Z. Benitez
Manila, The Philippines

UKOY
(Shrimp Fritters)

1 cup flour

1/2 teaspoon baking powder

1 egg, well beaten

1 clove garlic, finely minced

1 teaspoon salt

1/4 cup water or more

2 tablespoons annatto seed, soaked in 1/4 cup water, rubbed, and strained, or 1 tablespoon achuete powder (optional)

2 tablespoons spring onions, finely cut

1 cup tiny shrimp (fresh alamang), blanched and drained, or medium shrimp about 1 1/2 inches long

Oil for frying

Paprika

Mix all ingredients except shrimp, adding enough water to make a thick batter similar to pancake batter. Color with annatto water, if desired. Add alamang shrimp and blend well. Heat cooking oil and use a slotted spoon to drop into hot oil in a frying pan. Deep-fry on both sides until golden brown. Drain on a paper towel. If desired, dip hot fritters into a sauce of 1/2 cup vinegar, minced garlic cloves, salt, and pepper. Serve on a lettuce leaf as a main dish or an appetizer. Makes 2 dozen.

Note: If using medium shrimp, cut each in half lengthwise. Drop a few shrimp halves together into the batter and transfer them with a slotted spoon or fork to the hot oil. Proceed with a few at a time. When each fritter is turned, sprinkle with paprika. Fry each 2-inch fritter to a golden brown.

Linda C. Chincuanco
Manila, The Philippines

GINUMIZ
(A Gelatin Dessert)

1 cup toasted rice cereal (Asian or American)

1 cup nata de coco *(cubes of fermented coconut juice bottled in syrup)*

1 cup cubed red gelatin (cherry or strawberry)

1 cup cubed blue gelatin (Berry Blue)

Coconut cream mixed from a powder or a can

Sugar to taste

In a tall goblet, layer toasted rice, *nata de coco*, and gelatin cubes. Add water to coconut cream according to package directions (1 or 2 tablespoons), whip, and combine with sugar. Or use sweetened whipped cream. Add to the goblet.

To serve this dessert as a cool refreshment on Independence Day, top with crushed ice and decorate with miniature Philippine flags of red, white and blue the colors of the dessert. *Kaong*, white crunchy fruit from the coconut palm, can be added or substituted for *nata de coco*.

Susan C. Exconde
Manila, The Philippines

Red, white, and blue Ginumiz is popular on Independence Day.

Ukoy are fried fritters with tiny alamang shrimp unique to the islands.

CORN SOUP WITH SILI LEAVES

2 tablespoons cooking oil

1 teaspoon garlic, crushed

2 teaspoons onion, sliced

1 cup cooked pork, sliced

1/2 cup shelled shrimp

4 cups shrimp juice

1/8 teaspoon salt

Dash of pepper

1 cup fresh corn kernels, shredded

2 cups sili leaves (similar to jalapeño pepper leaves)

1 dozen quail eggs, hard-cooked and shelled

In oil, sauté garlic, onion, pork, and shrimp. Add shrimp juice, cover, and bring to a boil. Season with salt and pepper. Add corn, and, when cooked, add sili leaves and simmer for another 2 minutes. Correct seasonings to taste and, just before serving, drop peeled quail eggs into the hot soup. Serves 6 to 8.

Note: Shrimp juice can be made by pounding shrimp shells until very fine and washing with warm water through a sieve until 4 cups are obtained; discard the crushed shells.

Lydia Viajar
Manila, The Philippines

Sweden

On the weekend closest to June 24, happy Swedes celebrate the modern version of a prehistoric summer solstice. The festivities begin on Midsummer's Eve. Those who have not left town for weekend cottages or camping sites gather in city parks and village greens for games and dancing around the Midsummer Pole a descendant of the medieval Maypole brought to Sweden from Germany. Neighborhood residents who have spent the afternoon dressing the pole in its holiday garb of birch branches and flower circlets now gather around it for fiddlers' songs and ring dancing.

Children get in on the fun with afternoon competitions and traditional dances. But the evening — which darkens little in this northern land — is set aside for adults of any age to rejoice in dancing and merriment. The celebration continues all weekend as families everywhere get together in outdoor settings or at their garland-decorated homes to enjoy the summer sunshine.

The midsummer menu always includes delicate new potatoes, boiled with dill and splashed with butter, and herring — perhaps Matjessill, sweet-pickled and served with fermented cream and chopped chives. And, without fail, strawberries with ice cream or whipped cream. To drink, there is beer, schnapps, or the fermented milk called *filmjölk*.

Sweden is famous for its *smörgåsbord*, which again features herring and either salmon, trout, or *gravad lax* — fresh salmon marinated in vinegar, spices, and dill weed. Herring also shows up at the mini-buffet known as *smor*, with bread, butter and cheese, cold meats, smoked fish, and relishes. A legacy from the days of one-pot cookery are the still popular Swedish pea soup with pork and *kalops*, a beef stew.

SWEDISH POTATO SALAD

8 large potatoes, peeled and cut into matchstick pieces
3 tablespoons shredded leek
3 tablespoons finely chopped dill pickle
1 teaspoon seasoned salt
1/2 teaspoon ground white pepper
Mustard dressing
Capers

Place potatoes in boiling water; blanch until water returns to the boil. Drain and rinse with cold water. Combine potatoes, leek, pickle, and seasonings. Cover with mustard dressing and garnish with capers.

To make mustard dressing: Combine 3 tablespoons Swedish mustard, 1 tablespoon sugar, 1/2 cup white wine vinegar, 1 teaspoon seasoned salt, and 1/2 teaspoon white pepper. Mix 1 cup vegetable oil with 2 tablespoons water and, a few drops at a time, beat into the mustard mixture, increasing to a fine stream while beating vigorously so that the dressing does not separate. Serves 6 to 8.

Marie-Louise Jansson
Huddinge, Sweden

PICKLED HERRING

2 salted herrings
1/3 cup vinegar
2/3 cup water
1/2 cup sugar
2 red onions, peeled and sliced
1/2 teaspoon allspice
1/4 teaspoon peppercorns

Clean herrings, cut into fillets, and soak in deep water overnight or for 12 hours. Bring vinegar, water, and sugar to a boil and set aside to cool. Skin the fillets and cut into 1-inch pieces.

In a glass bowl, alternately layer herring pieces and onions and then sprinkle spices on top. Pour cooled vinegar mixture over all and refrigerate overnight before serving. Offer sour cream and chopped chives on the side.

SCANDINAVIAN PUFF

PASTRY

1 cup flour

1/2 cup butter

2 tablespoons water

PUFF FILLING

1/2 cup butter

1 cup water

1 teaspoon almond flavoring

1 cup flour

3 eggs

FROSTING

2 cups powdered sugar

2 tablespoons butter

1 1/2 tablespoons almond extract

5 tablespoons cream

1 cup slivered almonds, toasted

To make pastry: Preheat oven to 350° F. Measure flour into a bowl and cut in butter using a pastry blender or knives. Sprinkle the flour mixture with water and mix with a fork. Make a round ball and divide in half. Using fingers and the edge of a hand — the warmth helps to create pastry — pat the dough into two strips about 12 inches by 3 inches and place side by side on a baking sheet (ungreased). Set aside. Be patient in working the dough — it does work!

To make puff filling: Set a heavy saucepan over high heat. Combine butter and water and bring to a boil. Turn off heat, add almond flavoring and flour, and beat with an electric beater to prevent lumps. Add one egg at a time, beating well after each until the mixture is smooth. Spread over each strip of the dough on the baking sheet. Place pastries in the preheated oven and bake for about 60 minutes. Pastry will puff up slightly but shrink while cooling, leaving a custardy portion in each center. Cool completely.

To make frosting: Cream together sugar and butter. Add almond extract and enough cream to make an icing consistency — slightly drippy. Frost each half of the cooled dough and sprinkle with almonds. Cut on the diagonal and serve. Can be made a day ahead.

Rubye Erickson
Minneapolis, Minnesota

Herring, dill potatoes, and strawberries are the usual Midsummer lunch.

BRAZIL

4th Week of June
FESTAS JUNIAS
(JUNE FESTIVALS)

Festas Juninas, the monthlong celebration of three popular saints in the world's largest Roman Catholic country, stands in sharp contrast to Brazil's better-known festival. Carnival brings forth images of a giant theatrical production on a flowing stage, the pre-Lenten merriment of balls, masquerades, sizzling sambas, and riotous street parades.

The June Festivals honor St. Anthony on June 13, St. John the Baptist on June 24, and St. Peter on June 29. Many Brazilians return to their country roots on these weekends. Gathering in flag-bedecked front yards at dusk, celebrants dress in typical country clothing, the women in full skirts and matching blouses streaming with ribbons, the men in checkered shirts and rustic trousers strewn with patches, both beaming beneath traditional straw hats as they dance, watch fireworks, and greet friends around stupendous bonfires.

They might begin feasting Saturday at noon with everyone's favorite cold-weather lunch, Feijoada, a black bean stew originally prepared by slaves from pork parts rejected by their masters. Legend tells that it wasn't long before the masters borrowed and improved the recipe. Around the evening fire, they might eat corn on the cob, baked sweet potatoes, boiled manioc root, fruit, or a sweet such as Arroz Doce, rice pudding flavored with anise and cinnamon. Caipirinha, the national drink of lime or lemon and sugar cane liqueur, is always present. So might be Guarana, local berries of magical qualities ground into a powder and carbonated.

Carioca hosts in Rio might serve their Friendship Force visitors cosmopolitan dishes such as Shrimp with Cream Cheese; the creole cookery of old Brazil; or the popular gaucho cuisine of the south, especially Churrasco, skewered meat roasted over live coals. But everywhere one finds Feijoada! It is truly a national dish!

FEIJOADA
(Black Bean Stew)

1 1/2 pounds jerked beef, such as Italian dried beefstick
2 pounds salted pork ribs, smoked ribs, or a combination
1 pound thick pork sausages
1 pound other sausages: Portuguese, Spanish chorizo, or Polish kielbasa
1 1/2 pounds pork tenderloin, seasoned with salt and pepper
1 1/2 pounds fresh link sausages
2 pounds salted pork tails, ears, and feet (optional)
4 1/2 pounds black beans
10 ounces bacon, cut into small cubes
1 onion, chopped
10 cloves garlic, crushed
2 tablespoons oil

Soak any dried salted meats, if used, including optional tails, ears, and feet, in water for 24 hours. Change the water 3 or 4 times. Inspect and wash black beans and soak overnight. Next day, remove the meats, cut into 2-inch chunks (except optional pieces), and boil for 30 minutes. In another pan, boil the tails, ears, and feet until soft; debone the meat and save the water.

In a large, deep kettle mix black beans, meat cubes, and the three optional pieces. Cover with reserved water and cook for 4 hours, adding water as needed. In a saucepan, fry bacon, onion, and garlic in oil; if desired, add more onions and less garlic. Add to the stew pot, mix all ingredients well, and cook for 10 minutes over low heat. Just before serving, discard the tails, ears, and feet. Serve with white rice, *farofa* (golden fried manioc meal), chopped kale cooked like greens, and a platter of sectioned oranges. Serves 12 to 16.

Helena Shimomura
Campinas, Brazil

Caipirinha
(Shrimp with Cream Cheese)

1/2 lemon, smashed
2 teaspoons sugar
Pinga (sugarcane liqueur)
Ice cubes

In a small old-fashioned glass, mix lemon, sugar, and a dose of Pinga (1 or 2 shot glasses). Add ice cubes and it's ready to drink! Repeat for additional servings.

Herculano Passos
Campinas, Brazil

Camarão com Catupiry
(Shrimp with Cream Cheese)

2 pounds fresh shrimp, shelled
1/2 teaspoon salt
Juice of 2 limes
2 large onions, chopped
3 tablespoons chopped green olives
3 tablespoons olive oil
2 tablespoons fresh, chopped cilantro
3 tablespoons tomato paste
1 heaping tablespoon maize (cornstarch)

1 cup milk
16 ounces California cheese (cream cheese)
3 tablespoons Parmesan cheese

Marinate the shelled shrimp with salt and lime juice for 1 hour. Sautée onions and olives in oil until the onions are soft and transparent. Stir in cilantro. Add the marinated shrimp, cover, and simmer at low heat until cooked, about 10 minutes. Stir in tomato paste. Dissolve cornstarch in milk and add, stirring until the mixture bubbles. If necessary, add more milk and salt. Spread cream cheese in a glass baking dish and cover with the shrimp mixture. Top with Parmesan cheese and brown in a moderate oven until bubbling, about 30 minutes. Serves 6.

Anisia Quirino da Silva
Rio de Janeiro, Brazil

The flavors of Feijoada, Brazil's "national dish," result from long hours of cooking the black beans and meats.

Canada: Canada Day Desserts

 # CANADA

1st Week of July
CANADA DAY

On the second long weekend after summer weather appears in Canada, families across this vast country come together to enjoy Canada Day festivities, an outdoor concert or a barbecue picnic in the park — or perhaps to leave the city with camping gear.

Formerly called Dominion Day, this national holiday marks the passage of the British North America Act on July 1, 1867, which unified Upper and Lower Canada, New Brunswick, and Nova Scotia. As with most countries honoring their heritage, flags fly everywhere and parade routes are crowded. Late in the evening, after darkness finally comes to the far north, fireworks dazzle in every city and especially in Ottawa, where they give color to the night sky over Parliament buildings.

Fish and shellfish from sea and stream are true year-round favorites in Canada; salmon come from waters off both coasts, and Prince Edward Island provides lobster. In Newfoundland cod tongues and seal-flipper pie are delicacies, while small Winnepeg Goldeye fish make Manitoba famous. French-speaking Quebec offers a unique Christmas pastry with poultry, pork, and mushrooms called Parte de Noel. English food is popular in Ontario.

Two sweets named for the regions that made them famous are Fredericton Walnut Toffee, a candy brought by Loyalist settlers, and Nanimo Bars, first made in British Columbia. Together with fruit cobbler and carrot cake, they are popular desserts at family dinners and picnics on Canada Day. Mushroom Croustades is an appetizer that is perfect while waiting for the picnic to be assembled.

FREDERICTON WALNUT TOFFEE

1 cup or more chopped walnuts
1 cup (1/2 pound) margarine or butter
1 1/3 cups packed brown sugar
3/4 cup chocolate chips
1/2 cup or more chopped walnuts

Grease an 8-inch pan and cover the bottom with 1 cup or more chopped walnuts. Melt margarine over medium heat and add brown sugar. When the mixture starts to bubble, turn heat to low and cook for 12 minutes, stirring constantly. Pour over the walnuts, then sprinkle with chocolate chips. When they begin to melt and turn shiny, smooth the top with a spatula, then sprinkle with at least 1/2 cup more chopped walnuts. Cut into squares.

Note: Weather will determine softness; colder days result in a harder toffee than warmer days.

Gabrielle Mazeroile
Fredericton, New Brunswick, Canada

Carrot Cake makes its appearance on the Canada Day dessert table.

NANIMO BARS

1/2 cup butter or margarine

1/4 cup sugar

1 egg

4 tablespoons cocoa

2 cups graham crumbs

1 cup flaked coconut

1/2 cup chopped walnuts

4 tablespoons (1/4 cup) butter

3 tablespoons milk

2 tablespoons vanilla custard powder (pudding mix)

2 cups sifted icing sugar (powdered)

4 squares semisweet chocolate

1 teaspoon butter

Cream 1/2 cup butter and mix with sugar, egg, and cocoa. Set over boiling water, stirring until custard-like. Combine crumbs, coconut, and walnuts. Blend into the custard mixture. Spread and press into a pan about 9 inches square.

Cream 1/4 cup butter, milk, pudding mix, and powdered sugar. Spread over the pan mixture. Chill thoroughly. Melt chocolate over hot water; add 1 teaspoon butter and blend well. Spread over the top and let it set. Refrigerate.

Kathryn Williams
Ottawa, Ontario, Canada

RHUBARB-STRAWBERRY COBBLER

3/4 cup sugar

2 tablespoons flour

4 cups chopped rhubarb

1 teaspoon cinnamon

1 teaspoon grated orange peel

2 cups sliced strawberries

TOPPING

1 cup flour

2 tablespoons sugar

1 teaspoon baking powder

1/4 teaspoon baking soda

2 tablespoons margarine

2/3 cup buttermilk

Combine cobbler ingredients and spread in a 7″ x 11″ or 8″ square glass baking dish. Microwave for 10 minutes on high.

To make topping: Mix flour, sugar, baking powder, and soda. Cut in margarine until the mixture is the size of small peas. With a fork, stir in buttermilk until a soft dough forms. Drop by spoonfuls on the hot fruit in six evenly spaced mounds. Bake for 20 minutes in a 400° F oven, until the top is golden. If desired, top with sweetened whipped cream.

Barbara Warren
Lethbridge, Alberta, Canada

CARROT CAKE

2 cups flour

2 teaspoons baking soda

1 teaspoon salt

2 teaspoons cinnamon

1/4 teaspoon ground cloves

3/4 cup sugar

1 cup dark brown sugar, packed

1 1/4 cups salad oil

4 eggs

1/2 can (3 ounces) frozen orange juice concentrate, thawed

1 teaspoon vanilla

3 large carrots, shredded (3 cups or more)

1 cup chopped walnuts

1 can (8 ounces) crushed pineapple, drained

GLAZE

1/3 cup butter

2/3 cup sugar

1/4 cup buttermilk

2 tablespoons light corn syrup

1/2 teaspoon vanilla

Preheat oven to 350° F. In a large bowl, combine dry ingredients: flour, baking soda, salt, cinnamon, cloves, and the two sugars. Stir in the oil, eggs, orange juice, and vanilla. Beat at slow speed until well mixed, then beat at high speed for 5 minutes, scraping sides of the bowl toward the center several times with a rubber spatula.

Fold in the carrots, walnuts, and pineapple and pour into a greased and floured 9- or 10-inch bundt or other tube pan. Bake for 50 to 60 minutes or until a toothpick inserted in the center comes out clean. Cool for 10 minutes, then prick the top several times with a toothpick. Pour half the glaze over the top and cool for 15 more minutes. Remove from the pan and pour remaining glaze over the cake, allowing it to run down the sides. Or sprinkle powdered sugar on top, if preferred to a glaze.

To make the glaze: Melt butter and add sugar, buttermilk, and corn syrup. Bring to a boil, stirring, and simmer for 5 minutes. Add vanilla.

Lorraine Ziegler
Victoria, British Columbia

MUSHROOM CROUSTADES

2 tablespoons butter, softened

24 slices thin-sliced white bread

4 tablespoons (1/4 cup) butter

3 tablespoons finely chopped shallots

1 pound mushrooms, finely chopped

2 tablespoons flour

1 cup heavy cream

1/2 teaspoon salt

1/8 teaspoon cayenne

1 tablespoon finely chopped parsley

1 1/2 tablespoons finely chopped chives

1/2 teaspoon lemon juice

2 tablespoons Parmesan cheese, grated

Butter

With a pastry brush and soft butter, heavily coat the insides of 24 tiny muffin tins (each 2 inches across the top). Cut 3-inch rounds from the bread slices and press gently into the tins, pushing centers into wells and gently molding bread around the sides with a thumb or finger. Bake for 10 minutes at 400°F. Set aside to cool.

Melt 4 tablespoons butter in a heavy 10″ pan; before the foam subsides, add shallots. Stir over moderate heat for 4 minutes without browning; add mushrooms and mix well to thoroughly coat each. Stirring, cook for 10 to 15 minutes until moisture evaporates. Remove from heat. Sprinkle flour on the mushrooms and stir until flour is absorbed. Pour on the cream, stir and bring to a boil. When thick, reduce heat and simmer for 1 or 2 minutes longer. Remove from heat; add herbs, seasonings, and juice. Let cool and refrigerate.

In each croustade, mound the filling lightly; sprinkle with Parmesan cheese, dot with butter, and place the tin on a cookie sheet. Heat for 10 minutes in a preheated 350° F oven, then place briefly under the broiler. Do not allow to burn.

Kathryn Williams

MID-ATLANTIC STATES, U.S.A.

2nd Week of July
FOURTH OF JULY

Even today, the Mid-Atlantic region of the United States — which cradled and nourished a new democracy in 1776 — is rich with the sites and sounds of a nation being born. The original recipe for freedom — equal parts of brilliance, patriotism, and selflessness — still guarantees that Independence Day will come around each July 4th, the day in 1776 on which the Continental Congress formally adopted the Declaration of Independence.

Coming as it does in the middle of a hot summer, the 4th of July is most often a family day to be spent outdoors. The choices are many: a picnic in the backyard or day at the beach; the Capitol Fourth on the Washington Mall; fireworks over Baltimore's inner harbor and Ft. McHenry, where the national anthem was born; jazz festivals, pop concerts, and long-distance races; or one of the thousands of brassy parades that wind through the country. Perhaps the nation's longest-running one is held in Bristol, Rhode Island, a 4th of July event since 1785. In another long tradition, on the steps of the village hall in Fishkill, New York, the Declaration is read aloud to the citizenry as it has been since 1902.

The 4th of July calls for barbecued chicken, broiled steaks, hamburgers on the grill — and everything that goes with them: three-bean and potato salads, baked beans, lemonade or minted iced tea, old-fashioned hand-churned ice cream and cherry cheesecake — spread out on red, white, and blue paper tablecloths, centered by a scooped-out watermelon filled with the bounteous fresh fruits of summer.

It's always a happy and carefree day when American families get together to celebrate their national birthday. Evenings end with a softball game, perhaps, and a drive to the family's favorite spot to watch a sparkling rainbow of fireworks in a sky erupting from coast to coast with the fervor of America giving thanks.

Since America's original emancipation proclamation — the birth certificate for a nation — was drafted by Thomas Jefferson, it is fitting that each year on July 4th new Americans swear their allegiance and receive the mantle of citizenship on the steps of Jefferson's palatial home, Monticello.

It is also fitting that the city where independence first was celebrated Philadelphia — hosts the largest and most significant birthday bash. The first small observance in 1776 was followed in 1777 with the all-day tolling of bells, including the Liberty Bell, and 13-gun salutes from the harbor. Today the party honors descendants of the original signers — two of them lightly tap the venerable Liberty Bell 13 times, a signal for church bells to begin pealing throughout the country. Philadelphia's town criers then announce three nights of blazing fireworks and a host of festivities begins in America's most historic square mile.

CHARCOAL-BROILED FLANK STEAK

1/2 cup soy sauce

3 tablespoons Worcestershire sauce

3 cloves garlic, minced

5 dashes Tabasco sauce

1/4 teaspoon black pepper

1 1/2 pounds flank steak

Combine first 5 ingredients in a flat glass dish and add flank steak to the marinade, turning occasionally. Cover with plastic wrap and refrigerate while marinating for about 6 hours. Drain. Grill over charcoal for about 10 minutes on each side until cooked to taste. To serve, make 1/4-inch slices on the diagonal. Serves 6.

Frank Teetsel
Wayne, New Jersey

MARINATED POTATO SALAD

6 to 8 boiled potatoes (about 1 quart), diced
1/2 cup chopped celery
2 hard-boiled eggs, cut into chunks
2 tablespoons vinegar
2 tablespoons oil
1/2 teaspoon salt
1 heaping tablespoon chopped onion
2 teaspoons prepared mustard
1 teaspoon sugar
1/2 cup mayonnaise
Paprika

Prepare separately potatoes, celery, and eggs and set aside. Cook together until blended the vinegar, oil, salt, onion, mustard, and sugar. While hot, pour over the potatoes and marinate for several hours. Before serving, add celery, eggs, and mayonnaise. Sprinkle paprika on top. Optional: 1/2 cup chopped sweet pickles and 1/4 cup of their juice. Serves 6 to 10.

Jean Farneth and Ann Jones
Lancaster, Pennsylvania

GINA'S 3-LAYER BROWNIES

LAYER 1
3/4 cup cocoa
1/2 teaspoon baking soda
2/3 cup vegetable oil
1/2 cup boiling water
1 1/2 cups sugar
2 eggs
1 1/3 cups flour
1/4 teaspoon salt
1 teaspoon vanilla

LAYER 2
2 cups powdered sugar
8 tablespoons (1/2 cup) margarine, softened
3 tablespoons crème de menthe syrup

LAYER 3
1 cup chocolate chips
6 tablespoons margarine

Make layer 1: Mix cocoa, baking soda, and oil. Add boiling water, stirring until the mixture thickens. Add sugar and eggs and stir until smooth. Add flour, salt, and vanilla. Stir and pour into a greased 9″ x 13″ pan. Bake for 30 minutes at 350° F and cool.

Make layer 2: Mix powdered sugar, margarine, and crème de menthe syrup. Stir and spread over layer 1. Chill for 1/2 hour.

Make layer 3: Melt chips and margarine. Spread on top of the brownies. Chill again and cut into squares. Can be frozen before cutting; also can be served in cupcake papers. Makes about 24 squares.

Anne Witmer, Smoketown, Pennsylvania
Gina Plain, Lancaster, Pennsylvania

PINEAPPLE-SOUR CREAM-MARSHMALLOW SALAD

1 can (16 ounces) crushed pineapple
1 can (16 ounces) pears, drained and cut up
1 bottle maraschino cherries, drained and cut up
1 cup sour cream
1 cup marshmallows
1/2 cup shredded coconut

Mix all ingredients and let stand overnight in the refrigerator. Serves 6.

Frank Teetsel

GRANDMA GILBERT'S BARBECUED CHICKEN

1/2 cup vegetable oil
1 cup vinegar
1 tablespoon salt
1 1/2 teaspoons poultry seasoning
1/4 teaspoon pepper
1 egg
2 pounds chicken, cut up

Combine the first 6 ingredients, mix well, and add chicken pieces. Soak for 2 to 3 hours, or overnight. Broil over charcoal, turning and basting every 10 minutes. Cook for 1 hour or until chicken is tender and dark brown in color.

Jerry Gilbert
South Charleston, West Virginia

Three-layer brownies are an easy-to-make-and-take picnic dessert.

CROCK-POT BAKED BEANS

1 1/2 pounds (about 3 cups) dry navy beans
1 medium onion, chopped
1 cup ketchup
1 cup brown sugar
1 cup water or drained bean liquor
2 teaspoons dry mustard
2 tablespoons dark molasses
1 tablespoon salt
1/4 pound salt pork, diced

In a large saucepan, simmer dry beans in three times their volume of unsalted water for 30 minutes. Cover and allow to stand overnight. Next morning, make sure beans are soft, then drain and place into a Crock-Pot (slow cooker). Add other ingredients and mix well. Cover and cook on low for 10 to 12 hours — or at the high setting for 4 to 6 hours, stirring occasionally. Serves 24.

Note: Presoaked beans also can be cooked overnight in the Crock-Pot and warmed just before taking to the 4th of July picnic.

Shirley Dawley
Safety Harbor, Florida

FRANCE

As a tribute to the storming of the Bastille in 1789 in rebellion against the tyrannical Bourbon dynasty, the 14th of July has been a national holiday for Frenchmen since 1880. When the mob destroyed the prison fortress that summer day, it destroyed as well the absolute power of the king and brought forth the bloody French Revolution and liberty.

Today, as it did then, the tricolored flag flies in every village and throughout the capital city. While each town has a morning parade, the largest happens in Paris in the presence of the president. Fighter planes of the Patrouille de France (the French Patrol) draw blue, white, and red smoke in their wake. Enormous crowds watch the Tour de France bicycle race; if won by a Frenchman, the race is an inspiring 14th of July triumph. In the evening, fireworks dazzle the skies.

The average French family takes things easy on Bastille Day, perhaps with a picnic or dinner party that could last several hours — a popular pastime in a country where fine food is a way of life. The hostess might begin with Poule au Pot and follow with two entrées of lamb, veal, beef, or duck and a variety of vegetables. Last to come would be three or four cheeses and the rich pastries for which France is renowned — and of course the wines: an appetizer to begin, a good Bordeaux or Bungundy, and a sweet wine with dessert.

Poule au Pot makes a simple but popular meal in France, especially around Pau, where King Henry IV was born in a nearby chateau. Villagers say that the kind-hearted king proclaimed that every French family, however poor, should have a hen in the pot on Sundays. And so it continues today.

POULE AU POT
(Hen in the Pot)

A stewpan large enough so water will cover the hen
1 large farm hen
4 quarts water
Salt to taste
Flavoring bouquet: 1 or 2 twigs thyme, laurel (bay)
*   leaf, and parsley, tied with string*
Salt to taste

STUFFING
3 eggs
1 cup (4 ounces) bread crumbs, crumbled by hand or
*   blender*
Liver of the hen, minced
Thick slice of raw, salted Bayonne ham, chopped (or
*   bacon)*
2 cloves garlic, minced
2 tablespoons parsley, minced
Salt and pepper to taste

VEGETABLES
3 medium carrots
2 or 3 medium turnips, halved
3 or 4 leeks, or a small cabbage, quartered

Wash the hen inside and out. Mix stuffing ingredients, insert into the hen, and stitch the opening closed with a curved needle and fine string. Boil 4 quarts of water in stew pan and add the hen, flavoring bouquet, and salt. Cover and cook for 1 hour over moderate heat; remove residue on top as needed. Add vegetables and cook for 1 more hour. Check cooking time and seasoning. Remove hen and vegetables when tender, and discard the bouquet. Remove and slice the stuffing, carve the hen, and arrange both on a platter with the vegetables. Serve with French dressing, tomato sauce, or pickles according to taste. If desired, cook vermicelli for a few minutes in the hen broth, removing excess fat. Serves 6.

Roger Abeille
Pau, France

LAPIN AUX RAISINS

(Raisins Rabbit)

1 rabbit
2 onions, sliced
Butter or margarine
6 or 7 medium carrots, sliced
1/2 cup raisins
4 to 6 ounces red or white wine
Salt, pepper, and thyme, to taste
Mushrooms, peeled (optional)

Cut the rabbit into chunks or pieces. In a heavy saucepan or kettle, sauté onions in melted butter over brisk heat. Add rabbit pieces and turn in the hot butter until brown on all sides. Add carrots, then raisins and lower the heat. Add wine, enough water to cover, and seasonings. Cover the kettle and simmer for 75 to 90 minutes, according to the weight of the rabbit. If desired, add peeled mushrooms. Raisins Rabbit can be served with mashed potatoes and wine of choice. Serves 5.

Patrick Thinot
Compiegne, France

BLANQUETTE D'AGNEAU

(Lamb Blanquette)

8 lamb cutlets
1 onion, minced
2 tablespoons butter
1 tablespoon flour
5 or 6 cloves garlic
Flavoring bouquet: 1 or 2 twigs thyme, rosemary, and
*   parsley tied with fine string*
Salt and pepper to taste
1 cup (8 ounces) cold milk
1 tablespoon cider vinegar or lemon juice
1 egg yolk

In a frying pan, heat enough water to cover the cutlets. Just before it boils, remove from heat, add the cutlets, and leave a few seconds until the meat becomes colorless. Discard the water and wipe the cutlets. Fry the onion in a small amount of fat. Then add butter and flour, stirring gently. Add garlic, bouquet, salt, and pepper. While stirring over a moderate fire, add milk progressively. Add vinegar or lemon juice and continue cooking and stirring for a few more seconds. Add the lamb, check the flavoring by tasting, and cook for about 20 minutes. Remove from the heat and before serving stir in the egg yolk. Serve with rice, if desired. Serves 4.

Colette Peraldi
Pau, France

GRATIN DAUPHINOIS
(Potatoes au Gratin)

2 1/4 pounds potatoes

1 clove garlic to rub

2 cups milk

6 ounces Gruyère cheese, grated

1 egg, beaten

1/2 teaspoon salt

Black pepper to taste

4 tablespoons (1/4) butter

Nutmeg (optional)

Peel potatoes and cut into thin rounds. Place in a flat 9″ x 13″ ovenproof dish rubbed with a clove of garlic. Heat the milk and add 2/3 of the cheese, the beaten egg, salt, and pepper. Bring to a boil, pour over the potatoes, and bake in a moderate 350° F oven, covered, for 30 to 40 minutes. Uncover the potatoes and top with "au gratin" by sprinkling the remaining cheese on top and covering with melted butter. Continue to bake, uncovered, for 15 minutes or until the potatoes are tender. Option: Add a sprinkle of nutmeg from one turn on the grinder. Serves 6 to 8.

Denise Parganin
Engomer, France

Raisins Rabbit is cooked the French way in wine.

TARTE TATIN
(Apple Tart)

DOUGH

4 tablespoons (1/4 cup) butter, softened

1/3 cup sugar

1 egg

1/2 teaspoon salt

1 1/2 cups flour

FILLING

8 golden cooking apples

6 tablespoons butter, softened

1/2 cup fine sugar

Vanilla to taste

2 teaspoons rum flavoring

To make dough: Blend butter, sugar, egg, and salt. Add flour and mix with fingers to make a ball. Cover and refrigerate 1/2 hour. Peel the apples, remove seeds and core, and cut into 6 or 8 slices each. Thickly butter a round 10-inch pan, spread out the sugar, and fill with apple slices arranged close together. Sprinkle with vanilla and rum.

Dust a table surface with flour and flatten the dough to a circle slightly larger than the pan. Place on top of the apples, pressing the outer edges. Make a small hole in the center. Bake for about 50 minutes in a preheated 425° F oven, placing an aluminum sheet on top if the pastry gets too brown. Cool for 10 minutes, then invert onto a plate. Serve warm — alone or with custard, ice cream, or chantilly cream. Serves 6 to 8.

Therese Barthe
Pau, France

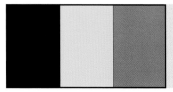

BELGIUM

4th Week of July
NATIONALE FEESTDAG
(INDEPENDENCE DAY)

Although Belgium is known as the hub of western Europe — with easy access to the most important cities — its location has caused Belgium to become a battlefield many times throughout its history. Surrounded tightly by France, Germany, Luxembourg, and the Netherlands, it often has been absorbed or assaulted by one neighbor or another.

Cultures intermingle, and it is not surprising that four languages coexist — French spoken in the southern half, Flemish in the north, and German in the east, with English as a fourth. Independence Day in this constitutional monarchy, which honors the day in 1830 when Belgium finally became an independent kingdom, is known as La Fête Nationale, Nationale Feestdag, and Nazionale Festdag — but is all the same day, July 21.

It is a happy day for Belgians, conquered so many times through the ages. Coming in the middle of summer, it's the perfect day for one of the glorious beaches that stretch 40 miles along the Atlantic — although some prefer the forests of the Ardennes. In Brussels, the capital city, military units parade before King Albert II and the famous Grand' Place is crowded with other Belgian families with the day off and anxious to dine out.

Native dishes in Belgium rival those of its neighbor, France. Dining at home is a fine art, with the use of famous Belgian linens and lace, full china service, and an array of crystal for the many beverages. Guests would be served cocktails, or apéritifs, followed by four full courses: a warm entrée like Turbot with Champagne Sauce; perhaps Frogs' Legs Soup with Spinach; a main dish like Rabbit with Thyme, and a dessert such as Charlotte of Chocolate.

Those who want a less formal family dinner on

the national day might choose Tomato Stuffed with Grey Shrimp from the Belgian North Sea or the popular Moules et Frites — boiled mussels with Belgian fried potatoes (not known here as French Fries) and a fresh, crusty bread. The vegetable might be the famous endive the world knows as Brussels sprouts or native-grown asparagus. To drink: a good red wine or strong local dark beer.

Martin Cobbaert and Manfred Ketschker of Germany drink a toast to each other's recipes.

TARBOT MET CHAMPAGNESAUS
(Turbot with Champagne Sauce)

2 pounds tarbot (turbot) fillets
1 tablespoon butter
1 pound tomatoes, crushed or diced
1 tablespoon parsley, chopped
1/2 bottle champagne
1 cup fresh cream
Salt and pepper to taste

Cut fish into sticks and place into a frying pan with butter, tomatoes, and parsley. Pour champagne over the fish and bake for 20 minutes at 350°–375° F. Allow the fish sticks to set a few minutes before placing on a platter. Add cream and seasonings to the sauce and pour over the tarbot. Serves 4.

Board Members
The Friendship Force of Brussels-Pujot, Belgium

MOULES MARINIÈRES

(Mussels)

4 1/2 pounds mussels
1 onion, cut into strips
2 tablespoons butter
1 1/2 cups dry white wine
1/3 cup fresh parsley, chopped
1 bay leaf
2 small sprigs thyme
Salt and pepper to taste
3 plum tomatoes, cut into chunks
2 tablespoons parsley

Clean mussels with a knife, scraping off anything attached to the shells, including beards. Discard mussels whose shells have opened. Wash the remainder in several changes of water. In a large saucepan, cook onion strips in melted butter until transparent. Add mussels, wine, parsley, herbs, salt and pepper. Stir well, bring to a boil and simmer for 10 to 15 minutes, shaking saucepan often and stirring, so mussels on the surface can go to the bottom to open. When most have opened, discard those which have not, and place the opened mussels in a large serving bowl or shallow platter. Keep warm. Add tomatoes to the juice and simmer for 3 more minutes. Pour over mussels and sprinkle with an additional 2 tablespoons parsley. Serves 6.

Rosa Borloo
Brussels, Belgium

CHARLOTTE VAN CHOCOLADE

(Charlotte of Chocolate)

9 ounces dark chocolate
1 cup black coffee, divided
2 tablespoons sugar
10 tablespoons (scant 2/3 cup) butter, softened
4 eggs, separated
Pinch of salt
2 heaping tablespoons castor (fine) sugar
30 sponge or lady fingers

Butter a glass bowl and set aside in a cool place. Melt chocolate with 4 teaspoons coffee in the top of a double boiler. Mix sugar and butter until creamy and add to the chocolate. Beat egg yolks, add to the mixture, and after a few minutes, remove and allow to cool. Beat egg whites and add salt. Sprinkle with fine sugar. Fold egg whites slowly into the cooled chocolate.

Dip each sponge finger quickly in the remaining coffee and line the sides and bottom of the bowl. Pour chocolate mousse into the bowl and add broken pieces of sponge fingers. Refrigerate for an hour and a half. Turn cake onto a cake plate and garnish with icing made from melted chocolate and powdered sugar. Top with sweetened whipped cream. Serves 6 to 8.

Note: Since neither the egg yolks nor whites are cooked in this recipe, it may be advisable to use pasteurized eggs.

Martin Cobbaert
Oetingen, Belgium

PERU

5th Week of July
FIESTAS PATREAS
(INDEPENDENCE DAY)

The people of Peru enjoy a rich heritage, with 45 percent of them Quechuan, descendants of the great Incan empire. On July 28, 1821, independence from Spain was declared by their revered leader and liberator, Jose de San Martin. Victory was complete by 1826.

Each year on July 28 and 29, Peruvians enjoy a two-day holiday to celebrate Independence Day. On July 28 they listen together to the president's speech on the state of the union and government proposals for the coming year. Families attend church services on the 29th and many gather for breakfast before going to Avenida Brasil to watch the military parade.

They return home for a typical midday meal of roast beef; Ceviche, a spicy raw seafood seasoned with lemon and vinegar; Arroz Verde Con Pollo, chicken with green rice; and seasoned fresh vegetables or the popular Papa a la Huancaina, which can be an appetizer or a side dish. In the evenings, they might visit a cafeteria for coffee or enjoy music, dancing, wines, and beer.

Patricia Torres Byrne of Lima, Peru, samples her cooking.

Friendship Force visitors to Lima feel most happily at home when their hosts proclaim, "Esta en su casa" ("You are in your house"). They come away extolling Peruvian hospitality, the focus on family life — and perhaps even the siesta!

CARNE DE ASADO
(Roast Beef)

2 cloves garlic, finely chopped
1 teaspoon salt
1/2 teaspoon each: pepper, paprika, and flavor enhancer
4 teaspoons vinegar
2 1/2 pounds rolled rump roast
4 small carrots cut into 1- to 2-inch lengths (or 8 to 10 baby carrots)
1/4 cup vegetable oil
3 cups water
1 beef bouillon cube
1 medium onion, sliced

In a bowl, mix spices and vinegar into a paste-like consistency. With a knife, punch holes in the beef and insert several carrot pieces. Coat the beef with the paste and marinate for 1 hour. Heat vegetable oil in a large pot or frying pan and brown meat on all sides. Add water, bouillon cube, onion, and remaining carrots. Bring to a boil, reduce heat, and simmer for 30 minutes uncovered. Remove the beef, carve into 1/2-inch slices, and return to the pan, simmering for 40 more minutes. Serve with white rice or garlic spaghetti.

Martha Comer
Lima, Peru, and Dayton, Ohio

PAPA A LA HUANCAINA
(Potatoes with Cream Sauce)

1 cup milk
10 saltine crackers
1/4 cup peanuts
1 or 2 hot peppers
1/4 cup chopped onion
2/3 cup feta cheese
3 hard-boiled eggs
3 tablespoons cooking oil
Garlic, salt, and pepper to taste
6 medium potatoes, boiled and peeled
6 large lettuce leaves

Combine milk, crackers, peanuts, hot pepper, onion, and feta cheese in blender and mix into a creamy consistency. Add one hard-boiled egg and the oil and blend. Mix in garlic, salt, and pepper.

Martha Comer prepares Carne de Asado.

Slice potatoes and remaining two eggs. Place a lettuce leaf on each of 6 salad plates and add sliced potatoes on each. Cover with the cream sauce and top with an egg slice. Potatoes in cream sauce can also be served on a platter. Serves 6.

Martha Comer

SOPA PILLAS
(A Pastry Dessert)

2 cups flour
1 teaspoon salt
1 teaspoon baking powder
3 tablespoons shortening
3/4 cup warm water
Vegetable oil for frying
Confectioners' sugar, honey, or jam

Sift dry ingredients together, cut in the shortening as for piecrust, add warm water, and mix well. Allow to stand for 30 minutes. Then roll out onto a lightly floured surface and cut into 2-inch squares. Drop each into at least 1/2 inch of hot oil in a frying pan and fry until golden, turning once after the first side browns. Lift out and drain on paper towels or brown paper. Roll each in confectioners' sugar — or, if preferred, make a slit on one side of each pilla and insert 1 1/2 tablespoons honey or a tablespoon of grape or strawberry jam.

Patricia Torres Byrne
Lima, Peru

~ AUGUST ~

Midwesterns Mary Bryant with Crown Roast of Pork

GHANA

1st Week of August
HARVEST FESTIVALS

The many tribes and clans of the West African nation of Ghana celebrate the harvest with festivals unique to each. In Accra, the capital, people from each clan's area of the city gather on a different day between late July and late August to give thanks for a good year and decide on improvements for the next.

On their Homowo Festival day in early August, the Ga clan goes to the ancestral stool house where the chief and elders pour a morning libation to toast clan ancestors. In the afternoon a parade down the area's main street includes drumming, dancing, and colorful floats. Dressed in full tribal regalia, Ga members walk behind their chief as he sprinkles food along the route — symbolically feeding their ancestors — before receiving homage back at the throne house. Families gather to share a meal before or after the parade.

For the Fanti clan the festival is called Odambea, which is celebrated in the traditional area of Nkusukum by all of its 25 towns. The week before festival, clan members make a mixture of mashed yams, palm oil, and eggs which the King of Nkusukum sprinkles around the stool house to ask for abundant food, good health, a good life, and a happy festival week. Other events follow, and on Saturday members wear ancestral clothing and gather to watch the King and Queen Mother of Nkusukum carried by on palanquins, followed by the Kings and Queen Mothers of the 25 towns. Drumming and dancing and gaiety fill the air.

The official program includes greetings from Ghana officials, a review of the past year, and suggestions for the next, after which the King and Queen Mother each host a party deep into the night and receive homage from the extended family of Fantis. On Sunday the chiefs attend a thanksgiving service at either the Methodist, Episcopal, or Roman Catholic church.

GROUND NUT SOUP AND STEAMED RICE

3-pound chicken, cut into 10 pieces
1 piece fresh ginger, peeled and shredded
4 cloves garlic, finely chopped
1/3 cup tomato paste
1 teaspoon salt
2 quarts water
3 or 4 jalapeño peppers, boiled 5 minutes and puréed
1 medium onion, chopped
8 ounces ground-nut paste (peanut butter)
1 cup water
4 medium tomatoes, boiled 5 minutes, peeled and puréed

Wash chicken pieces and place in an 8-quart stew pan. Season the chicken with a blend of ginger, garlic, tomato paste, and salt and cook dry over moderate heat until the chicken is lightly browned. Add 2 quarts water and the peppers and onions. Mix ground-nut paste and 1 cup water with a wooden spoon or blender to form a creamy sauce. Add to chicken broth and boil for 10 minutes. Add blended tomatoes and boil for 20 minutes. Turn heat down and simmer for 10 minutes until oil comes to the surface and the soup thickens. Serve with steamed rice.

Elizabeth Arthur
Accra, Ghana

Akwadu is a popular baked banana and coconut dessert.

KPEKPELE
(Steamed Cornmeal)

6 cups coarse stone-ground cornmeal
1/2 cup water or more
1 cup red palm oil, warmed
1 cup okro (okra), puréed and salted (optional)

Ghanians begin preparation of Kpekpele following the previous year's harvest, when corn kernels are cut from cobs and spread to dry. During festival week the dried corn is soaked in water for 3 days until it ferments. Then it is taken to the mill.

To make Kpekpele, put coarse cornmeal in a bowl and sprinkle with water to dampen. Smooth with the hands, pack down, and set aside. The next day, place a layer of cheesecloth over a small-holed colander (or top of a double vegetable steamer). Fluff the cornmeal with the fingers and put 1/3 into the cheesecloth. Spread and fold remaining cheesecloth over it. Cover and steam over moderate heat for about 15 minutes. Set aside and repeat twice more. When all is well cooked, remove kpekpele to a saucepan and fluff again. Pour palm oil a little at a time over and around the cornmeal and gently mix with the fingers until it becomes smooth and yellow. Mound in a serving bowl and provide small bowls for each person's desired use: pour Palm Nut Soup (below) over it; eat as a side dish, or scoop from a bowl of puréed okra and blend into the Kpekpele. Serves 6 to 8.

PALM NUT SOUP

5 pounds of beef, chicken, or lamb, cubed

1 cup chopped onions

6 cups palm nuts or 1 can (30 ounces) palm nut sauce

5 jalapeño peppers

1 large onion, cut into pieces

4 tomatoes, sectioned

2 quarts water

Smoked fish pieces (optional)

Cut your choice of meat into 1/2-inch cubes. Brown lightly in its own fat, add chopped onions, and steam for 10 minutes. Meanwhile, cook palm nuts in water. When cooked, remove pulp and pound with mortar and pestle until the seeds separate. Sieve the pounded pulp into a bowl, discard seeds, and set aside.

In a saucepan, cook peppers, onion chunks, and tomato sections until soft. Process in the blender, then return to the saucepan, add the palm nut pulp, and blend with 1 to 2 cups water to a creamy consistency. Blend in the remaining water and add the meat mixture. Cook together for 10 minutes or until the meat is tender. If desired, add fish pieces (only with beef or lamb) and cook for another 15 minutes until palm oil comes to the surface and the soup has thickened. Serve in a large tureen and share with friends and visitors. Serves 10 to 12.

Veronica Asante
Accra, Ghana

In 1989, Elizabeth Arthur, president of The Friendship Force of Ghana, was approved by the people of Nkusukum to be their Queen Mother under the name of Nana Egyima I. An impressive ceremony was held in Salt Pond, central city of Nkusukum, to honor her new lifetime title.

AKWADU
(Baked Bananas and Coconut)

4 or 5 small bananas, halved lengthwise

4 tablespoons (1/4 cup) butter, melted

2 tablespoons lemon juice

1 cup orange juice

1/2 cup light brown sugar

1 cup shredded coconut

In a lightly greased 7″ x 11″ ovenproof dish, arrange peeled banana halves to cover the bottom. Pour melted butter, then mixed juices over the bananas. Sprinkle first with brown sugar, then with coconut. Bake for 12 minutes in a 350° F oven or until the coconut is golden. Serve warm in individual bowls.

Elizabeth Arthur

MIDWESTERN STATES, U.S.A.

2nd Week of August
STATE FAIR WEEK

State Fair! What excitement it generates in the Midwest each year from mid-August to early September . . . when the sweet corn is ripe . . . when farm animals are groomed and ready to compete . . . when the pacers and trotters are anxious to be hitched to sulkies for the harness races . . . when the apple butter and vine vegetables are in finest form for the judges . . . when the midway is set up, brassy and gleaming in the sun. It's harvest time all through the heartland!

Since the mid-19th century, State Fair has been the perfect way for families to end a busy summer and celebrate the finest blessings from the earth and from the efforts of farmers red-faced from hours in the sun.

Harvest festivals are an inheritance from the earliest days when agriculture was the primary livelihood of man. Harvest Home festivals are still a part of parish life in England; Michigan's National Cherry Festival and Floralies in Beligum are among those which salute particular harvests.

The staggering amounts and varieties of foods produced on the vast midwestern farmlands long ago proved the adage that these states are not only the geographical center of the country, but the heart of its agricultural sustenance as well.

Midwestern families are the beneficiaries of all this bounty. When a clan gathers for a meal — whether picnic style at State Fair or at home — there might be a beautifully crowned roast of pork, cinnamon apples, puffy herbed biscuits, crunchy cornbread sticks, steaming bowls of fresh vegetables, and a dessert table laden with pumpkin, mince, and cherry pies and homemade caramel apples. Iced tea, first introduced at the 1904 World's Fair in St. Louis, and fresh apple cider wash it all down.

Corn on the cob reigns supreme in the Midwest — succulent, sugar-sweet, dripping with butter. The shucked ears must come directly from field to ready pot of boiling water to table. There's no finer treat, or finer way to salute a harvest, than corn on the cob in mid-August in America's breadbasket.

HARVEST MEAL IN A MILKCAN

Ruth Starkey of The Friendship Force of Greater Des Moines, Iowa, calls her milk-can meal a variation on the cast-iron Dutch oven meal of early settlers. A Dutch oven is still an option today, although the milkcan makes an ideal cooking pot for a large crowd.

Potatoes, peeled or in jackets — one per person
Whole carrots
Small onions or onion slices
Desired seasonings: salt, pepper, garlic, etc.
Freshly picked sweet corn, husked, with silks rubbed off
1/2 cup hot water
Bologna-ring sausage

Scrub and sterilize one milk or cream can, 2 to 3 feet tall. Heat the can on an outdoor fireplace until it is VERY hot to the touch. If a rack is used, the fire should be very close to the bottom of the can.

In layers, place ingredients in the can as listed. Place a bologna-ring sausage on top. In Iowa this is known as a Pella or Amish sausage, although link sausages can also be used. Sausage flavors the corn as it cooks and the juices flow down onto the corn layer. Place the lid on the can, thereby sealing it.

Cook over the fireplace with a constant hot fire for

at least 1 1/2 hours. Cooking time, however, depends on how many vegetables have been added. If the can is very full, it may be an all-afternoon task. Check the ingredients occasionally with a long-handled fork. When vegetables are tender, carefully remove the milkcan from the heat and allow it to cool before opening the can. Can serve as many as 24 to 30.

Serve with fresh cucumbers; harvest slaw with cabbage, green pepper, and onion rings; sliced tomatoes from the garden; garlic bread; or baked butternut squash.

Ruth Starkey,
Des Moines, Iowa

CROWN ROAST OF PORK WITH APPLE-SAUSAGE STUFFING

Loin of pork formed into a crown roast
8 ounces lean, whole-hog pork sausage
4 tablespoons (1/4 cup) butter or margarine
1 cup diced onion
2 cups diced celery
8 cups of 1/2-inch bread cubes, spread overnight to dry
3 chicken bouillon cubes
3 cups boiling water
1/4 teaspoon marjoram
1 teaspoon crumbled sage leaves
1/8 teaspoon black pepper
Dash garlic powder
2 medium unpeeled Winesap or Jonathan apples,
  cored, finely diced

Ask the butcher to form and tie the pork loin into a circular crown with rib bones outside, meaty portions inside. Place the pork in a large roasting pan; cover rib ends with foil to prevent over-browning. Put the roast in a preheated 450° F oven, then immediately reduce the temperature to 350° F. Roast until a meat thermometer reaches 160° F; remove the roast and fill the center with apple-sausage bread stuffing. Return to the oven and continue baking until a temperature of 175° F is reached, about 1 additional hour.

To make stuffing: Break up pork sausage and fry in a skillet until well cooked. Remove, drain on a paper towel, and crumble when cool. Discard grease from the skillet. Add butter and sauté onions and celery until almost tender. Place dry bread cubes in a large bowl. Dissolve bouillon cubes in boiling water; pour only enough over bread cubes for a soft consistency. Add spices, diced apple, crumbled sausage, onion, and celery. Lightly mix and adjust seasonings to taste. Place mixture in the center of the partially cooked crown pork roast and continue baking. Serves 8.

To serve: Carefully remove the stuffed roast to a platter and surround with spiced apple rings. Replace foil wraps on the ribs with white parchment "boots" — available in a cookware shop or rolled from 1-inch by 4-inch fringed strips.

Mary Bryant
Lincoln, Nebraska

Ruth Starkey shows the ingredients for her unique milkcan meal.

CORN STUFFING BALLS

1/2 cup chopped onion
1 cup chopped celery
4 tablespoons (1/4 cup) butter
1 can (16 ounces) cream-style corn
3/4 cup water
8-ounce package herb-seasoned stuffing mix
3 egg yolks
1/2 cup melted butter

Cook onion and celery in butter until tender. Add corn and water. Bring to a boil and pour over the stuffing mix. Blend lightly and mix in egg yolks. Shape into balls and place in a shallow baking dish. Pour melted butter over all. Bake for 15 to 20 minutes in a preheated 375° F oven. Serve warm. Makes 16 to 18 corn balls.

Marilyn Frick
Bettendorf, Iowa

ROASTED VEGETABLE SALAD

1/3 cup white balsamic vinegar
2 tablespoons olive oil
2 or 3 cloves garlic, crushed
1 teaspoon dried Italian seasoning
1/2 teaspoon each: salt and pepper
2 teaspoons molasses
1/2 pound carrots, peeled and thinly sliced
1 sweet red pepper, seeded and cubed
1 green bell pepper, seeded and cubed
2 zucchini, sliced
1 yellow squash, sliced
1 large onion, cut into eighths and layers separated

Combine first 6 ingredients in a bowl and set aside. Combine vegetables and add to the vinegar mixture. Let stand for 30 minutes, stirring occasionally. Drain vegetables, reserving the vinegar, and arrange on a shallow, rimmed cookie sheet. Bake for 30 minutes in a 450° F oven until tender and beginning to brown, turning occasionally. Return vegetables to the reserved vinegar mixture and toss gently. Cover and refrigerate for at least 8 hours. Serves 6 to 8.

Sheri Leonard
Wichita, Kansas

PICKLED BEETS WITH SLICED ONIONS

2 cans (8 ounces each) sliced beets
1 cup plus 4 tablespoons vinegar
1 teaspoon salt
Dash of powdered clove
2 small bay leaves
2 small onions, thinly sliced

Drain beets and reserve 1/2 cup of the liquid. Place beets in a bowl. In a saucepan, combine beet liquid and all other ingredients. Bring to a boil and simmer for 5 minutes. Pour over the beets and refrigerate for at least 1 hour before serving.

Marie Gray
The Friendship Force of Missouri

HUNGARY

3rd Week of May
ST. STEPHEN'S DAY

St. Stephen was the founder of the Hungarian monarchy in A.D. 1000 and a strong and revered leader who brought Christianity to the Magyars. The national holiday on August 20 that bears his name also is known as Constitution Day and is the official state festival.

Since St. Stephen's Day comes in late summer, it is also the day for celebrating the new bread after the harvest; one old custom is to bake a small twist of bread and place a candle in it at the holiday dinner of family favorites. In addition to church services, there also are cultural events, street dances, family excursions, and fireworks, especially in the capital, Budapest.

Other special days are Independence Day on March 15, dating from the 1848 freedom fight against the Hapsburgs of Austria — and Republic Day on October 23, a modern holiday tradition which marks the 1956 revolution of discontent and also the eventual proclamation in 1989 of the Republic of Hungary.

A country situated at the crossroads of the continent, Hungary is a blend of European influence, Magyar inheritance, peasant traditions, and remnants of the Huns, Franks, and Slavic peoples who migrated there. Their cuisine includes elements of them all, and they consider eating a real delight.

Onions, garlic, and the famous red paprika, either sweet or hot, give Hungarian foods their definitive flavor. Sour cream enriches every dish, from soups and sauces to vegetables and pastries.

Palacsintas are thin crepes stuffed with meat to begin a meal, or made with chocolate to finish it. Wines from the northern shore of Lake Balaton, Eger, or a small village in northern Hungary called Tokay are all deservedly famous.

Geraniums form the backdrop of Hungarian food ready to cook.

HUNGARIAN POT ROAST

1/4 pound bacon, minced
5 onions, diced
2-pound beef roast
Salt
3 cans (6 ounces each) tomato paste
1 teaspoon minced garlic
1/2 teaspoon marjoram
1/2 teaspoon black pepper
1/4 cup white wine
2 tablespoons sour cream

Brown bacon pieces and remove. Cook onions in bacon fat, add a little water, cover, and cook slowly until they are caramelized. Salt the beef well on all sides and let stand for 1/2 hour. Add tomato paste, minced garlic, and bacon bits to the onions; cook at slow heat. Meanwhile, brown the beef well on all sides and place in the tomato paste mixture.

Cover and simmer for 2 hours or until tender. Remove beef to a serving dish. To the sauce add marjoram, black pepper, white wine, and sour cream. Mix and serve over the beef. Both can be served over rice.

Zita Tibold
Pecs, Hungary

ZITA'S RICE

2 cups pineapple juice
1 cup golden raisins
2 chicken bouillon cubes
1/2 teaspoon salt
1 heaping tablespoon parsley
1 medium onion, diced
1 tablespoon cooking oil
1 cup rice

Mix the first 6 ingredients and bring to a boil. Add 1 tablespoon oil to the rice and cook slightly. Add liquid mixture to the sautéed rice, cover, and cook slowly until rice is tender, about 20 minutes. Mix and serve on the side.

Zita Tibold
Pecs, Hungary

APRICOT LEKVAR MERINGUE

3 cups flour, sifted
2/3 cup sugar
2 1/2 teaspoons baking powder
8 tablespoons (1/2 cup) butter or margarine
1/2 pint sour cream
3 egg yolks, beaten
1 teaspoon vanilla
8 ounces apricot lekvar jam (thick preserves)
3 egg whites
6 tablespoons sugar
Walnuts or pecans, finely chopped

Mix flour, sugar, baking powder, and butter as for a piecrust. Add sour cream, beaten egg yolks, and vanilla and mix together thoroughly. With a spoon or fingers, pat into a 9″ x 13″ oblong baking pan. Carefully spread apricot jam on top of the pastry, using a wet table knife. Bake in a preheated 350° F oven for 45 minutes. Remove. Beat egg whites until stiff, adding sugar a little at a time. Spread the meringue on top of the baked cake and sprinkle with chopped walnuts or pecans. Return to the oven for about 10 minutes, until the meringue browns lightly.

Note: If lekvar jam is not available, use apricot preserves: strain out any juices or cook down to a thicker jam.

Marian Oroszi
Fairborn, Ohio

LEKVAR

(Apricot Jam)

Thoroughly wash 2 pounds ripe, sweet apricots, cut in half, remove stones, and put in a large pan. Add $2^1/3$ cup sugar and stir to make sure apricots are coated with sugar. Cover and allow to stand for half a day, stirring occasionally. Bring the apricot mash to the boil, stirring often and simmer for 10 to 15 minutes, until residue disappears. Add 1/2 teaspoon salicyl (optional) and mix well. Put into sterilized jam jars and close tightly. Leave to cool in a dry steam: put the hot jam jars into a box stuffed with old rags or newspapers or other heat insulator. Leave until they are cool.

Judit Kavasy
Lakhegy, Hungary

PACIFIC NORTHWESTERN STATES, U.S.A.

4th Week of August
A SALMON BAKE

A legacy from the ancient river people of the Pacific Northwest is the delightful salmon bake, a happy outdoor event that satisfies the locals' love of the natural beauty and lush resources that surround them.

Salmon is not only the most nutritious and delicious of all fish but important to the diet of many generations of northwest Indians and the settlers and fur traders who predated 20th-century city dwellers.

Even today, in late August or early September, Indian tribes such as the Yakima and Wy-am herald the return of the first salmon from the ocean, the first huckleberries on the slopes of nearby Mount Adams, the first deer meat, and the first elk — in a ritual that is spiritual in feeling and meant to show respect for the earth and all its creatures.

The tradition of the salmon bake is an ideal way to entertain and enjoy nature in late summer in the Northwest. Each family has its own favorite way to prepare salmon — marinated and grilled, baked, attached to planks against an open wood fire, or even made into a salmon loaf or an appetizer ball.

Most often salmon is baked over charcoal in a backyard or park. With it comes corn on the cob or other seasonal vegetables, Indian fry bread, fresh fruits, and the wines of the region.

Residents of Oregon and Washington consider part of their heritage to be the apples from their orchards, the spices and herbs that can be grown year-round in the coastal climate, and the fish from the sea.

Speelyi, the legendary Indian god who created it, would agree that salmon has been the greatest of these gifts from the sea — for the Ancient People and for today's residents along the shores of the salmon's Pacific home.

SALMON IN INDIAN LEGEND

SPRING SALMON HAVE ALWAYS BEEN SACRED TO THE INDIANS OF THE PACIFIC NORTHWEST, AND EACH TRIBE KEEPS ITS OWN LEGENDS. MOST BELIEVE, HOWEVER, THAT A COYOTE GOD NAMED SPEELYI CREATED SALMON FOR THE PEOPLE OF WAUNA, THE GREAT RIVER OF THE WEST, NOW THE COLUMBIA. LEGENDS TELL HOW HE TAUGHT THE ANCIENT PEOPLE TO CATCH THE SALMON IN GREAT NETS MADE FROM THE ROOTS OF SPRUCE TREES, AND HOW TO CLEAN, DRY, AND SMOKE IT OVER A RACK. THE TRIBAL CHIEF AND HIS SHAMANS WOULD THEN SPEAK TO THE SALMON'S SPIRIT BEFORE IT WAS BAKED UNDER THE OPEN SKY ON A POINTED ARROW-WOOD STICK SLANTED OVER A BED OF COALS.

Beautiful Holmes Harbor and Puget Sound set the scene as Dolores Fresh and Terry Walters arrange picnic food for The Friendship Force of Whidbey Island in Washington State.

BARBECUED SALMON IN LEMON AND WHITE WINE

1 cup (1/2 pound) butter, melted
1 lemon, sliced
1 medium onion, thinly sliced
1 teaspoon chopped dill weed
1 cup white cooking wine or sherry
4 to 5 pounds whole salmon fillet
Garnish: sliced lemon and parsley

In a shallow baking dish, layer butter, lemon slices and onion slices. Sprinkle with dill, pour wine over the layers, and place the salmon on top.

Adding alder to charcoal on the barbecue grill is a northwest tradition which gives salmon a wonderful flavor. When coals are hot, place the pan on the grill. Every 5 minutes baste the salmon with cooking juices. Bake for 15 to 20 minutes or until the salmon is flaky. Garnish with additional lemon slices and parsley. Serves 6 to 8.

Dolores Fresh
Langley, Washington

INDIAN FRY BREAD
(An Old Cherokee Recipe)

2 cups warm water
1/4 cup sugar
1 package or 1 tablespoon yeast
3 cups flour, divided
3/4 teaspoon salt
2 tablespoons margarine, melted

In warm water, dissolve sugar, then yeast. Add 2 cups flour and salt. Stir until the dough is smooth. Add remaining flour and beat well. Add margarine and beat thoroughly until well mixed. Let the dough rise until double in volume. Press chunks of dough into 4-inch circles about 1/4-inch thick. Fry in one inch of vegetable oil in an electric skillet or frying pan at high heat, approximately 400° F. Cook on one side until puffed; then turn to the other side and repeat. Serve with margarine, honey, cinnamon sugar, or jam. Serves 6 to 8.

Bertieann Peters
Kelso, Washington

Resplendent salmon awaits its lemon and wine marinade.

Artha Saty shows how easy it is to make huckleberry pie.

PASTA SALAD

2 cups penne pasta (small, tubular)
1 1/2 cups broccoli flowerets
1/2 cup sun-dried tomatoes, reconstituted
1 yellow pepper, chopped
1/4 cup chopped red onion

DRESSING
1/3 cup balsamic vinegar
2/3 cup extra virgin olive oil
Dash of salt
1/4 teaspoon black pepper
3 cloves garlic, minced

Boil pasta for 11 to 13 minutes. Combine the broccoli, tomatoes, pepper, and onion in a large serving bowl. Separately combine the dressing ingredients and add to the pasta, then toss with the vegetables. Chill before serving.

Dolores Fresh

HUCKLEBERRY PIE

1 1/2 cups sugar
4 tablespoons cornstarch
1/4 teaspoon each: salt, nutmeg, and cinnamon
4 cups huckleberries
2 tablespoons lemon juice
1/2 cup water
2 tablespoons butter
2 tablespoons vanilla
Whipped cream, sweetened

PIE PASTRY
1 cup flour
1/2 teaspoon salt
1/2 cup shortening or margarine
1/2 cup cold water

To make the pastry: Combine flour, salt, shortening or margarine, and cold water. Roll out on a flour-dusted surface to a circle at least 11 inches. Lift and fit into a large 10″ deep-dish pie plate, fluting the edges and piercing the bottom and sides several times with fork tines. Bake in a preheated 400° F oven for 15 minutes or until light golden brown. Set aside to cool.

In a saucepan, mix sugar, cornstarch, salt, and spices. Fold in half of the berries, and add lemon juice and water (omit water if berries have been frozen). Bring to a full boil. When thick, remove from heat and add butter and vanilla. Fold in the remaining berries — this gives a fresher, whole-berry taste. Pour into the baked and cooled pie shell, top with sweetened whipped cream, and chill for 2 hours before serving.

Artha Saty
Spokane, Washington

Czech Republic: Beef and Cream Sauce

GREAT LAKES STATES, U.S.A.

1st Week of September
LABOR DAY

The end of summer unofficially arrives on the first weekend of September, the day set aside by Congress in 1894 to honor the workers — from explorers and settlers to builders of industry and tradesmen — who forged the links that created a nation.

Many countries celebrate Labor Day in early May, but it was never so in America; the September weekend is the only one considered for labor's sake. It is apropos, especially in the northern tier of states, as Labor Day gives workers one last long weekend of relaxation before the color-filled days of autumn and a few lazy ones of Indian summer lead into a tough winter.

Peter Maguire, founder of Labor Day, sought to recognize the industrial spirit which is "the great force of every nation" when he proposed a long holiday for the working classes in 1882. Perhaps Maguire's idea was borrowed from neighbor Canada, where labor rallies began in 1872 and where Labor Day also became official in 1894.

From its inception, founder Maguire envisioned street parades, picnics, and festivals as the most appropriate way to celebrate. Most Americans choose to spend the day outdoors, not only at civic parades and backyard cookouts, but also with excursions to the beautiful lakes, mountains, and seashores with which America is blessed.

In states bordering the Great Lakes, the key word is "labor" and the prevention of it for the housewife who prepares informal lakeside excursions: the most popular dishes easily can be prepared in advance or cooked by someone else on the grill.

At nightfall, fun in the sun changes to languid evenings lit by grills or bonfires. At Indian Lake in Ohio, and elsewhere in these lake-dotted states, cottagers light flares at eventide to make a ring of fire around the lake.

As it reflects in the water, it signifies the circle of friendship and family which makes Labor Day special.

THE LABOR DAY STYLE

LABOR DAY PICNIC TABLES ARE COVERED INFORMALLY WITH BEACH TOWELS, RED-CHECKED LINENS OR GAILY FLOWERED PAPER CLOTHS. THE CENTERPIECE MIGHT BE ANYTHING FROM A COLORFUL POT OF AUTUMN CHRYSANTHEMUMS TO THE RED, WHITE, AND BLUE OF AMERICAN FLAGS, STRAW BASKETS OF MULTI-HUED NAPKINS, OR HALF A WATERMELON HOLDING THE CUT FRUITS OF SUMMER. CRUSTY BREADS, RIPE HOMEGROWN TOMATOES, AND FRESH CUCUMBERS, PORTABLE DESSERTS, AND TUBS OF ICE-COOLED DRINK CANS COMPLETE THE SCENE. PAPER PLATES AND CUPS ARE NECESSARY FOR THE AVOIDANCE OF EXTRA LABOR.

GRILLED LAMBURGERS

2 pounds extra lean ground beef
1 pound ground lamb
3 large cloves garlic, minced
2/3 cup minced onion
2 tablespoons sour cream
1 teaspoon salt
1 teaspoon ground black pepper
Feta or blue cheese

Calico Beans includes four kinds of beans, bacon, and onions.

Mix all ingredients in a large bowl, but don't over-mix. Gently form into 12 burgers. Grill for 5 minutes on each side, depending on the coals. Test for desired doneness. Top with cheese and allow it to soften slightly. Serve on buns with thinly sliced onions and tomatoes.

Carole Janning
New Carlisle, Ohio

OTHER GRILL SUGGESTIONS

From an area heavily influenced by German immigration, roasted bratwurst on buns is suggested by Doris Mesenbrink of Lake Geneva and Jean Nethery of Richfield, Wisconsin. Chickens barbecued on a spit is the favorite of Claudia Pickens' family in Gahanna, Ohio, while Meg Tomlin of Libertyville, Illinois, chooses barbecued beef on buns.

CALICO BEANS

4 slices bacon, chopped
1 onion, chopped fine
1 can (16 ounces) kidney beans, drained
1 can (16 ounces) lima beans, drained
1 can (16 ounces) pork and beans
1 can (16 ounces) butter beans
1/2 cup brown sugar
2 tablespoons Worcestershire sauce
1/4 pound American or Cheddar cheese, cubed
1/3 cup ketchup
Parmesan cheese, grated (optional)

Brown bacon and onion; remove from heat and drain. Stir together all beans and other ingredients except Parmesan cheese. Place in a greased casserole and sprinkle with Parmesan. Bake in a 300° F oven for 45 to 60 minutes. If too dry, add a little of the reserved bean juice. Serves 12.

Catherine Clark
Dayton, Ohio

COLD CHERRY SOUP

1 cup sugar

1 cinnamon stick

3 cups cold water

2 cans (16 ounces each) pitted sour cherries, drained

1 tablespoon cornstarch

Hot water

1/3 cup heavy cream, chilled

3/4 cup dry red wine, chilled

1/2 cup dairy sour cream

A quartet of "cooks" from the Great Lakes states discusses their their favorite barbecues: left to right, Helen Mollere, Jean Nethery, and Catherine Garst of Wisconsin, with Meg Tomlin of Illinois.

In a 2-quart saucepan, combine the sugar, cinnamon stick, and water. Bring to a boil. Add cherries, partially cover, and simmer on low for 10 minutes. Remove and discard the cinnamon stick. Make a paste with cornstarch and hot water and blend into the cherry mixture. Stir over medium-high heat until boiling. Reduce heat and simmer for 2 minutes until the soup is clear and thick. Refrigerate until chilled. At serving time, add heavy cream, wine, and sour cream. Stir until smooth and serve. Serves 6 to 8.

Helen Mollere
Monona, Wisconsin

HOT FUDGE SUNDAE SAUCE

3 squares (1 ounce each) unsweetened chocolate

1 3/4 cup light cream or canned evaporated milk

1 1/2 cup sugar

1/4 cup flour

1/4 teaspoon salt

1 tablespoon butter

1 tablespoon vanilla

1/2 cup chopped nuts

Labor Day picnics seem to require a lake, and Carole Janning arranges to grill her Lamburgers at water's edge.

Melt chocolate squares in the cream. Cook until smooth, stirring occasionally. Combine sugar, flour, and salt, and add enough chocolate mixture to make a smooth paste. Add to remaining chocolate mixture and cook until smooth and slightly thick. Remove from the heat and stir in butter and vanilla. Serve hot or cold over ice cream, with a sprinkle of nuts on top.

Catherine A. Garst
Madison, Wisconsin

FRENCH PEAR PIE

5 large Bartlett pears (not too ripe), peeled and sliced
3 to 4 tablespoons frozen orange juice, thawed
Grated rind of 1 lemon
1 unbaked 9-inch piecrust

STREUSEL TOPPING
3/4 cup flour
1/2 cup sugar
1/8 teaspoon salt
1 teaspoon cinnamon
1/2 teaspoon ginger
5 tablespoons (about 1/3 cup) butter or margarine

Toss pear slices with the orange juice and lemon rind. Arrange in an unbaked pie crust. Mix streusel ingredients until crumbly and sprinkle over the pears, being careful to cover all the fruit. Bake at 400°F for 40 minutes or until the pears are tender.

Maggie Dohm
Middleton, Wisconsin

Peanutty Rainbow Cookies include coated chocolate candies, with or without nuts.

PEANUTTY RAINBOW COOKIES

1/2 pound (1 cup) margarine
1 cup peanut butter
1 cup packed brown sugar
1 cup white sugar
2 eggs
1 1/4 cups flour
1 teaspoon baking soda
1/2 teaspoon salt
2 1/4 cups uncooked oats
1 cup coated chocolate candies

Beat together margarine, peanut butter, and sugars until light and fluffy. Blend in eggs. Combine flour, soda, and salt; add to the mixture and blend well. Stir in the oats and candies. Drop by spoonfuls onto a greased cookie sheet and bake in a preheated 350° F oven until lightly browned.

Maggie Dohm

CHILE

The red, white, and blue of the Chilean flag provides the color and Chilenos provide the fervor when spring arrives in this far South American country. It is time once again to celebrate the first national government, dating from 1810, and independence from Spain after almost three centuries of domination.

In preparation for the two-day event on September 18 and 19, schoolchildren are made aware of its historical importance and eagerly anticipate their family's participation. Early on the 18th, flags and banners sprout from homes and public buildings; church services of thanksgiving draw crowds; and the president addresses the nation. Long-ago heroes of the revolution are saluted by students and the armed forces as they march through city squares in every community. And the family gathers: to decorate backyards with red, white, and blue garlands and to prepare favorite old family dishes.

Government officials, *huasos* from the countryside, and ordinary citizens gather in parks everywhere to stroll by temporary stalls called *ramadas* or *fondas* — palm-roofed structures of pine, eucalyptus, or other logs, decorated with flags and matching ribbons. Inside, red and white carnations deck the tables and Independence Day's traditional dishes are available, especially Empanadas and the popular dessert, Mote con Huesillos. In other *ramadas*, wines and foodstuffs are for sale.

The most popular are those resounding with folk music. Happy toasts might be made with Chilean red wine, Pisco Sours, a punch made with wine and sliced peaches, or Chica, a lightly fermented drink of cooked grapes grown on the mountainsides overlooking Santiago.

Throughout the nation, Chilean music and the familiar strains of La Cueca, the national dance, draw adults and happy children alike. It's a giant party, and Los Chilenos everywhere gather to enjoy it.

CAZUELA DE AVE
(Chicken Soup)

1 medium chicken, deboned, cut into small pieces
6 cups boiling water
2 tablespoons oil
6 potatoes, quartered
1/2 cup string beans, halved
6 pieces pumpkin, bite-size
4 tablespoons rice
1/4 teaspoon salt
1/8 teaspoon each: black pepper, cumin, oregano, and parsley
2 eggs, beaten (optional)

Put chicken pieces and water into a large saucepan and simmer over moderate heat. When chicken is half-cooked, remove and strain the broth. Add oil to the kettle and sauté chicken pieces, potatoes, string beans, pumpkin, and rice. Add the broth, herbs, and seasonings; simmer until tender. If desired, break 1 beaten egg into the serving bowl or tureen before adding the hot soup. Serves 6.

Graciela Wilson and Sonia San Martin
Santiago, Chile

EMPANADAS DE HORNO
(Meat Turnovers)

DOUGH
4 cups flour
1 teaspoon baking powder
1 teaspoon salt
1/2 pound (1 cup) margarine or lard
2 egg yolks
Water

Sift flour, baking powder, and salt. Pile onto a work surface. Make a well in the center and pour lukewarm fat into it. Work in quickly with fingertips, adding egg yolks and enough water — perhaps as much as 2 cups — to make a soft dough. Knead until it does not stick to the hands. While the dough rests, make the filling.

FILLING
1 pound chopped sirloin or other lean beef
3 tablespoons oil
4 to 6 small onions, chopped
1/2 cup raisins, soaked in warm water
Seasonings: salt, pinch of sugar, oregano, black
  pepper, and cumin
1/2 cup black olives
4 hard-boiled eggs, sliced
1 beaten egg for glazing

Chop meat into very small pieces and brown in oil. Add onions and cook for about 10 minutes, stirring often. Add drained raisins and seasonings; cook the mixture until onions are soft. Filling can be thickened with 1 tablespoon flour dissolved in 1/4 cup water, if needed. Allow to cool.

Separate the dough into 20 portions. Roll each portion into an 8-inch circle and fill each with 1 or 2 tablespoons of the meat filling, one olive, and one slice of hard-boiled egg. Fold in the middle, overlap the edges and seal well, folding over about 1 inch. Brush each turnover with the beaten egg. Place on a greased cookie sheet and bake at medium heat for 30 to 45 minutes. Serve in an entrée dish or simply onto a napkin in the hand. Serves 12.

Angela Rodriguez
Viña del Mar, Chile

ENSALADA CHILENA
(Chilean Salad)

Salted water
2 onions, sliced
4 tomatoes, sliced
Salt and pepper to taste
Oil, or a dressing of vinegar, oil, parsley, and coriander

Pour salted water over onion slices and let stand for 5 minutes. Drain and add to sliced tomatoes. Season with salt and pepper and a little oil. Or toss the tomatoes and onions with seasoned vinegar and oil dressing.

MOTE DE HUESILLOS

12 dehydrated peaches
1/2 cup sugar
1 cup mote *(hulled wheat or regular barley)*
Pinch of salt

Soak dried peaches overnight in cold water. Next day, add sugar and more water if needed to cover the peaches. Cook until soft, cool, and refrigerate.

Wash the *mote* with running water. Cover with fresh water, following directions on the package. Add a pinch of salt and cook in a saucepot until soft. Drain and cool. To serve, place 1/3 cup of the cooked mote in a dessert bowl or tall glass, top with one or two peaches, and cover with peach juice. Serve very cold.

Angela Rodriguez

KOREA

3rd Week of September
HARVEST MOON FESTIVAL

Korea's lunar moon holiday — translated as Chu Seok or Autumn Night — falls on August 15 in the eighth month of the lunar calendar, in mid- or late September on the western one. On this day families dress in new clothes to visit ancestral graves or to pay their respects at a home ceremony. In the evening, dressed in their best clothes, everyone gathers for a traditional Korean meal and to enjoy the most beautiful full moon of the year. In country areas, they enjoy community activities, including wrestling for the men.

The harvest festival meal — served most often at traditional dining tables close to the floor — might be charcoal-grilled beef, pork, or fish, with many vegetables and rice. Song Pyun, a special dessert served only on this gala day, is a rice cake containing newly harvested products like nuts and sweet red or yellow beans, which is steamed over pine needles. The entire family, even those visiting, joins in making it. Later family members unite around the cake for a Lunar Day ceremony which thanks their ancestors and the gods of nature for this and future bountiful harvests. Additional desserts might be Bam Kyung Dan (Chestnut Balls) and fresh fruits.

Korean food remains unchanged in spite of the nation's westernization. Steamed rice is served with a variety of meat and vegetable dishes. The most common dish is Kimchee, a highly seasoned, fermented pickle dish containing several vegetables. Soups of seaweed, meat, or fish are part of every meal, and a marinated beef dish called Pulgogi is popular. A special custom for many families is to offer the festive Green Pea Pancakes to guests on Harvest Moon night.

Chang Ki Sook serves Steamed Short Ribs to her family on Harvest Moon Festival night.

STEAMED SHORT RIBS

4 pounds beef short ribs

5 cups water

1 pound radishes, sliced into 3/4-inch rounds

10 Shiitake mushrooms, sliced

4 tablespoons green onion, white parts, chopped

2 tablespoons chopped garlic

1/2 cup soy sauce

2 cups pear juice

1/2 tablespoon sesame powder

2 tablespoons sesame oil

5 tablespoons sugar

1 pinch of pepper

6 chestnuts

10 gingko nuts

1 egg, separated

Remove fat from the ribs, make slit marks to the bone, and rinse off any blood. Boil in 5 cups of water until fatty parts are cooked and the oil floats freely; remove, keep warm, and save the stock.

Place sliced radishes in a saucepan, add ribs, and marinate with the condiments (next 9 ingredients) for about 10 minutes. Add 2 cups of stock to the marinade and boil for 20 minutes over moderate heat. Finally, add chestnuts, ginkgo nuts, and 2 more cups of stock. Simmer for 20 minutes or until ribs are tender. Place the beef on a platter, cover with sauce resulting from the cooking and decorate with egg bits: fry the egg white very thin, do the same with the beaten yolk, then cut both into very small diamond shapes. Serves 5 to 6.

Chang Ki Sook
Seoul, Korea

CHAPCHAE
(Beef Stir-Fry)

4 ounces sirloin or other lean beef
6 ounces dried pyogo or Shiitake mushrooms
1 each, cut into thin strips: medium onion, small
* cucumber and medium carrot*
2 ounces mung bean sprouts
1 egg
3 ounces tangmyon (Chinese noodles)
1 tablespoon pine nuts, with tips removed

SEASONINGS
1 tablespoon soy sauce
1/2 tablespoon sugar
1 teaspoon each: minced scallions and garlic
1 teaspoon each: sesame salt and sesame oil
1/4 teaspoon black pepper

Cut beef into thin strips. Soak mushrooms in hot water for 20 minutes, remove any stems, squeeze out excess water, and cut into thin strips. Mix the seasoning ingredients, add beef and mushrooms, and stir-fry in an oiled pan. Remove to a separate plate. Proceed to stir-fry other ingredients, removing each to a plate: onions, cucumbers which have been sprinkled with salt 10 minutes before, and carrots which have been parboiled and drained. Remove heads and tails of bean sprouts, parboil stems in salted water, drain, and stir-fry. Set all aside and keep warm.

Separately beat egg yolk and egg white. Pour yolk into a lightly greased pan and tilt to make a thin sheet; repeat with egg white and cut both into thin strips. Cook noodles as directed, cut into smaller pieces, and mix with sesame oil and soy sauce to taste.

Combine prepared ingredients and adjust seasoning to taste with sesame salt, sesame oil, and sugar. Arrange on a serving dish and decorate with egg strips and pine nuts.

Kyu Ok Kim
Seoul, Korea

BAM KYUNG DAN
(Chestnut Balls)

20 chestnuts
1 tablespoon honey
3 tablespoons sugar
1/4 tablespoon salt
1/2 cup water
5 tablespoons finely chopped pine nuts (divided)
1/2 tablespoon cinnamon

Mix chestnuts, honey, sugar, salt, and water in a pot and heat until a syrupy resin coats the chestnuts — 15 to 20 minutes. Skim off the foam and set aside. When cool, prepare chestnut balls: for white balls,

Chapchae (left) accompanies a plate of Panfried Zucchini and Ggochi-jon, squares of finger-size sticks of meat, green onion, and pepper held together with toothpicks and panfried.

roll half the chestnuts in 2 1/2 tablespoons of pine nut powder. For a different flavor and a black ball, roll the other half of chestnuts in a mixture of 2 1/2 tablespoons of pine nut powder and the cinnamon.

Chang Ki Sook

BIN-DAE-TTOK
(Green Pea Pancakes)

2 cups dried green peas
1 cup ground beef or pork
1 cup water
Salt and black pepper to taste
1/2 garlic clove, crushed (optional)
1 small onion, finely chopped
2 tablespoons vegetable oil
2 cups bean sprouts
4 green onions, cut into 3/4-inch lengths and split

DIPPING SAUCE
2 tablespoons vinegar
1/2 cup soy sauce

Soak dried peas in water overnight in the refrigerator. Drain and, if needed, remove any skins. Put into a blender with 1 cup water and process at slow speed for 1 minute. Lightly season the meat with salt and pepper and mix in the crushed garlic, if desired. Combine the meat, onions, and pea mixture in a bowl; season lightly as needed.

Heat a frying pan and add 1/2 tablespoon vegetable oil. Place 1 large scoop (1/4 the batter) in the oil and spread out with a spoon to make a 5-inch pancake. Place 1/4 of the bean sprouts and green onions on the batter. When the bottom is brown and cooked, flip pancake over to fry other side. Flip again back and forth, adding oil as needed. Repeat with other 3 pancakes.

As an appetizer, place each pancake on a plate and offer dipping sauce in a separate saucer. Eat with chopsticks or knife and fork. Makes 4 servings.

Duk-Won Yu Kim
Seoul, Korea

CZECH REPUBLIC

4th Week of September
ST. WENCESLAS DAY

On the weekend before September 28, families in the Czech Republic honor their patron saint and protector, St. Wenceslas — a 10th-century prince who was slain by his brother in 929. Even after his death, the young country united under his banner, which became the symbol of Christian Bohemia. His "wake" is still celebrated in the countryside, where towns and villages often hold religious services, followed by Posviceni, a fair with Czech folk music, dancing, and feasting.

The heartiest celebrants are those many Czechs who are named after Wenceslas (Vaclav) — such as President Vaclav Pavel and Prime Minister Vaclav Klaus. For them, dinner parties with friends, family, or co-workers make their "name day" special.

The traditional dinner for St. Wenceslas Day is Roast Goose, as popular here on patron saint days as in other East European countries. Kolaches, the well-known round cakes incorporating poppy seeds, cottage cheese, plums, or apples, are called "wake cakes" on this feast day. Family meals for the Czechs often feature roast beef with sour cream gravy and cranberries; pork with cabbage or sauerkraut, and always dumplings.

Special foods are connected with most Czech holidays. Carp is traditional for Christmas Eve and lentils are significant for the New Year. For Easter, small cakes are baked in the shape of lambs, and eggs are dyed brightly with Czech designs.

Other special days are Jan Hus Day on July 6, named for the Czech reformer and philosopher in whose memory bonfires are lit, and Independence Day on October 28, denoting the day Czechoslovakia was created in 1918 — a rebirth and union of two ancient Slav peoples, who peacefully separated again in 1993 into two autonomous nations.

KNEDLIK
(Dumplings)

3 cups fine white flour
2 teaspoons baking powder
1 egg
Salt
3/4 cup or more milk or water
2 baked rolls, cut into small cubes
2 tablespoons fat or oil

Sift together flour and baking powder; add egg, salt, and liquid. Work the dough until it is smooth. Lastly, add cubes of rolls which have been gently fried in oil. Divide the mixture and form into 2 loaves, each about 2 inches in diameter. Put into a large saucepan of boiling, lightly salted water. Boil for 20 minutes; halfway through, turn the dumplings over. Remove and cut into 1/2-inch slices.

Karel Vosatka
Prague, Czech Republic

VEPROVA PECENE
(Roast Pork)

2 1/4 pounds pork — shoulder, chops, or spareribs
2 or 3 cloves garlic
Salt
1 teaspoon caraway seeds
2 medium onions, chopped
Flour

Clean the pork. Crush the garlic and mix with salt to make a paste; sprinkle with caraway seeds and spread on the pork. Put into a roasting dish with the onions; add enough water so the pork does not singe.

Cover and stew in a hot 475° F oven for 15 minutes, then turn the heat to 350° F. While it is stewing, baste and turn the meat. When almost tender, remove the cover and continue roasting until well done and red-brown, about an hour. If more drippings are needed for gravy, brown some additional pork or bacon and add to the pan drippings. Thicken juices with flour mixed with a little water to make a paste. Serve with dumplings and cabbage.

Karel Vosatka

SVICKOVA
(Beef and Cream Sauce)

3 carrots
1 stalk celery
1/4 pound bacon
3 sprigs parsley
2 large onions, chopped
2 pounds beef roast or sirloin
Salt to taste
15 peppercorns
10 grains whole allspice
3 bay leaves
3 tablespoons thyme
1 cup water
Cranberry preserves

CREAM SAUCE
2 cups cream or half-and-half
Flour to thicken
1 teaspoon vinegar or grated peel from 1 lemon
Salt and sugar to taste

Clean carrots and celery and chop finely into long thin strips. Fry the bacon. Add carrots, parsley, and celery and sear for a few minutes. Add onions and cook until lightly browned. Then salt the meat to taste and add with the spices, which have been tied together in a spice bag. Add water and simmer over low heat, adding more water as needed.

When tender, remove meat from the heat. Remove vegetables and put through a thick sieve or blender. Remove spice bag and discard.

Add cream mixed with a little flour to the meat juices in the pot and thicken. Add vinegar or lemon peel and salt. Simmer, add sugar to taste, and thicken as needed. Carve the meat and arrange on a platter. Serve with cream sauce and top with cranberry preserves. Can also be served with dumplings or noodles.

Hanna Lochmanova
Prague, Czech Republic

ZELI
(Cabbage)

1 small cabbage
1 large onion
Salt to taste
A pinch of caraway seeds
Flour
Vinegar and sugar (optional)

Clean the cabbage and cut into quarters; remove the center stalk and chop the cabbage into long thin strips. Finely chop the onion and blend with the cabbage. Add salt, caraway seeds, and enough water to stew. Cook until cabbage is soft, and thicken juices with flour mixed in cold water. If desired, add vinegar and sugar to taste.

Janmila Radoza
Prague, Czech Republic

Turkey: Eggplant Kebabs

SLOVAKIA

1st Week of October
FAMILY WINE-TASTING

As the geographical center of Europe, Slovakia has been central to major history events since the first stone-age settlements. It is a country of abundance: picturesque mountains, rivers, and lakes; healing springs; rich folklore and architecture, including 270 medieval castles; and extensive wine-making areas. Predominate in its flag are red for the state, blue for the mountains, and a double white cross for Saints Cyril and Methodius in gratitude for their gift of Christianity.

A new era began for Slovakia on January 1, 1993, when Bratislava became the capital of the Slovak Republic after decades of Soviet influence and a forced federation with the Czech Republic. Centuries-old traditions survived through these years, including the custom of family-owned vineyards on the slopes of the Carpathian mountains, in backyards, or on rented strips of land that are long, narrow, and one row of vines deep. Most families have a garden plot, grow what they eat, and drink what they make.

Slovak families are close and meet often. Those with vineyards gather the generations together for the harvest; children cut the grapes, dropping them in baskets on the shoulders of their parents, aunts, and uncles. Other family members transport and press the grapes or clean, fill, and plug the barrels. After the wine has rested in the cellar for five days, the family reconvenes to taste the new wine and eat favorite foods like Kapustnica, Langose, or roast goose with potato patties.

The grape vines came with Roman settlement along the Danube. An early medieval etching shows church spires, grazing cattle protected by enfolding mountains dotted with grape vines, and a fishing boat on the Danubius — a picture in miniature of southern Slovakia today.

KAPUSTNICA
(Pork and Sauerkraut Soup)

1 pound smoked pork loin
3 pounds sauerkraut, washed and drained
2 ounces dried mushrooms, washed
6 ounces pitted prunes
1/2 cup vegetable oil
1 large onion, chopped
2 tablespoons or more flour
1/2 teaspoon sweet paprika
1/3 cup warm water
Salt and black pepper and 2 bay leaves
1/2 whole garlic bulb, crushed
1 pound Kielbasa sausage with garlic, thinly sliced
1 cup sour cream

Wash the pork, add enough hot water to cover, and cook for 20 minutes. When tender, add sauerkraut, mushrooms, and prunes. Cook for another 15 minutes. In vegetable oil, sauté onions and add enough flour and paprika to make a browning (similar to a roux). When brown, mix with warm water.

Remove the pork from the soup and cut into thin slices. Combine salt, black pepper, garlic, and bay leaves and add to the sauerkraut mixture on the stove. Bring the soup to boiling and stir in the browning. Simmer for 30 minutes more, stirring often. Add the sliced sausage and pork, season to taste, and cook for another 5 minutes. To serve, ladle into soul bowls and top with sour cream, if desired. Serves 4 to 6.

Helga Dingova
Bratislava, Slovakia

LANGOSE
(Fried Bread)

2 cups milk
1 ounce (4 packets or equivalent) dry yeast
1 teaspoon sugar
2 cups flour
Salt to taste
1 egg
1 potato, boiled and mashed
Vegetable oil for frying

Warm the milk and add yeast and sugar and set aside. When leavened, add to a mixture of flour, salt, egg, and mashed potato. Mix well and set aside for 30 minutes to rise. Divide the dough into 4 or 5 portions. With the hand or the back of a spoon, flatten each part into a 6- to 8-inch round. In a frying pan, cook each flat cake in hot oil on both sides. Serve with a sprinkle of garlic salt or a cheese slice, or form a sandwich by filling two of the fried bread cakes with a mixture of browned ground pork, onions and spices (paprika, salt and pepper, and chili powder, as desired).

Martin and Vera Sebeska
Bratislava, Slovakia

JABLKOVÝ TAHANÝ ZÁVIN
(Strudel)

1 1/2 cups flour, sifted
1/2 teaspoon salt
1/2 teaspoon powdered sugar
1/2 cup warm water
2 tablespoons vegetable oil
Melted butter or margarine

FILLING

1 cup sugar
1/2 cup raisins or currants
1/8 teaspoon nutmeg
1 tablespoon ground poppy seeds
6 cups apples (5 or 6), chopped fine
4 tablespoons (1/4 cup) butter, melted
Optional: 1 teaspoon cinnamon
1/2 cup chopped walnuts
Powdered sugar (optional)
Whipped cream

To make dough: Mix the first 5 ingredients until the dough sticks together. Knead lightly until it is smooth and creates bubbles. Shape into a ball and allow to rest in a warm place for 15 to 30 minutes.

Arrange a 30-inch square linen towel or tablecloth on a table and anchor it with tape. Sprinkle with flour. Place dough on the floured surface and roll toward the edges until it is about 1/8-inch thick. Lift dough carefully, place hands underneath and stretch the dough farther until it is very thin. Cut off any excess on the sides. Spread melted butter over the dough.

While oven heats to 375° F, combine the filling ingredients and arrange along the bottom edge of the dough. Fold in the uneven edges on each side. Lifting the tablecloth edge, roll dough up as with a jelly roll. Seal the ends and place the strudel roll, seam-side down, on a greased baking tin. (For a shorter pan, divide into 2 rolls, turning under all edges to seal.)

Bake until golden brown, for half an hour or more. Remove and sprinkle with powdered sugar, if desired. To serve, cut into slices and top with whipped cream.

Katarína Chlapíková
Bratislava, Slovakiá

GERMANY

2nd Week of October
25TH WEDDING ANNIVERSARY

As in most countries, a Silberhochzeit (silver wedding party) in Germany is a special occasion for family, relatives, and neighbors. Often couples will repeat the menu which was served at their wedding, with the original attendants and minister as honored guests at an evening party at home or in a restaurant. The music will vary from songs popular 25 years ago, to rousing German beer-drinking songs and today's music for the youngsters. There are always toasts and speeches about the couple's life together.

The party may begin with a noon luncheon for invited guests or at three in the afternoon with dessert and coffee. It continues through hilarious salutes by the children to their parents; dinner with several meat courses, many vegetable dishes and sumptuous desserts; a festive evening of dancing; and a lavish midnight buffet of cold meats and cheese, smoked fish, fruits, and salads. With it all goes beer, schnaps, Jagermeister, wine, and juices. Sometimes family and neighbors join the couple the next day for more toasts and mounds of leftovers.

In Germany the bride wears a silver crown and the groom a bouquet from a myrtle branch. In country towns, garlands of silver flowers and greenery are made and hung by neighbors. The village orchestra might serenade the couple. Sometimes a shower, like that for a new bride, is held the night before and includes the smashing of dishes for good luck in the next 25 years.

Flowers, silver candles, and champagne are profuse at a Silberhochzeit. Dishes are traditionally German or regional, the familiar ones on which the family was raised. In the spring, a favorite is home-grown white asparagus with ham and Sauce Hollandaise; in the summer, fresh trout with boiled potatoes and green salad; in the fall, Klopse und Gänsebraten (Dumplings with Roast Goose) and for winter, Rouladen, or Roast Pork with Prunes.

Dessert will be a decorated cake, fruit tarts, or — in season — Erdbeere mit Sahne (Strawberries with Whipped Cream). Rhabarber Grutzi (Rhubarb-Strawberry Jelly) is a favorite in Schleswig-Holstein and the Rhineland.

A silver wedding party in a northern Germany village begins with a family photo before the decorated doorway, and proceeds with a long evening of fun and food.

THÜRINGER KARTOFFELSALAT

(Thüringian Potato Salad)

4 1/2 pounds small new potatoes

2 strips bacon, crumbled

1 onion, chopped

Salt, pepper, and caraway seed to taste

1/2 cup sweet gherkin pickle cubes

1/4 cup pickle juice

2 cups yogurt

Boil potatoes in their jackets for 20 to 30 minutes. While still firm, peel and cut into small pieces. Brown bacon until crisp and add onion. Combine with the potatoes, salt, pepper, and caraway seed. Mix in gherkin pickle cubes and juice. Then add yogurt and mix well. Serves 8.

Serve with Thüringian charcoal-grilled sausages or meatballs made from ground pork, ground beef, onion, an egg, mustard, ketchup, and any desired seasonings — pepper, salt, caraway and/or rubbed nutmeg.

Christine Legner
Jena, Germany

SPARGELSUPPE MIT KRABBEN

(Asparagus Soup with Shrimp)

1 pound white or green asparagus

1 medium mealy potato

4 cups (2 cans) chicken broth

Salt and pepper

1/2 cup whipping cream

1 bunch chervil or parsley

1 cup shrimp, cooked

Clean asparagus and cut into inch-long pieces. Peel and cube potato. Add both to boiling chicken broth and simmer for 15 minutes. Remove vegetables from the broth. Set aside asparagus tips. Put remaining asparagus and potatos in a blender; when smooth, return them to the broth. Season with salt and pepper. Fold in cream. Chop chervil and add to the soup with the shrimp and asparagus tips. Warm and serve immediately. Serves 4.

Helga Mangels
Norderstedt, Germany

ROULADEN MIT ROTKOHL

(Meat Rolls with Red Cabbage)

*6 slices lean beef, about 7″ x 10″ x 1/4″, thin enough
    to roll*

Salt and pepper to taste

Brown German mustard

1 small onion, chopped

1 large dill pickle, cut into 6 long slices

6 slices lean bacon

Vegetable oil

5 cups boiling water

Salt beef slices on both sides and spread brown mustard on one side. Place onions, pickle slices, and a bacon strip at one end of the mustard side and roll like a jelly roll. Tie together firmly with string. Place the rolls in hot oil and fry on both sides. Add 5 cups boiling water, cover and simmer for 1 hour. Thicken remaining juices with cornstarch mixed with a little water, stirring until thick.

ROTKOHL

1 large head (10 cups) red cabbage, shredded

1 teaspoon caraway seeds

Juice of 1 lemon (3 tablespoons)

2 tablespoons red wine vinegar

4 tablespoons vegetable oil

3 tablespoons sugar

1/2 cup finely chopped onion

2 tablespoons apple juice

2 tablespoons fresh lemon juice

1 cup grated, unpeeled tart apple

1 to 1 1/2 teaspoons salt

Combine cabbage, caraway, lemon juice, and vinegar. Marinate overnight or for 10 hours in the refrigerator. Place oil and sugar in a saucepan and cook over medium heat until the sugar begins to turn brown. Dissolve, add onion, and stir. Add the cabbage mixture, apple juice, lemon juice, and apple. Stir, season to taste, lower heat, and simmer for 1 hour.

Marianne Miehe
Berlin, Germany

SOLEIER

(Eggs Boiled in Salt Walter)

In former times, the saltworkers of Halle made eggs boiled in salt water, which they were allowed to sell — a custom which prevails today. Manfred Ketschker has adapted this old recipe and serves it with dinner or with a glass of beer in the evening. Salt-water eggs in a jar are often found on the counter of a German bar.

12 eggs

1 onion

6 cups water

1 cup salt

2 small onions, peeled

2 laurel (bay) leaves

10 dried pimento berries (allspice)

3 juniper berries

1 teaspoon caraway, pulverized

1 stick thyme

6 cups water

Boil eggs in their shells with 1 onion for 8 to 10 minutes. (Adding a little salt to the water will prevent spillage if an egg is cracked.) Temper them with cold water and set aside to cool.

Combine all other ingredients in water, bring to a boil and allow to cool. Peel the cooked eggs and place in the brew. After 24 hours, they are ready to serve — whole, cut into halves, or sliced, with salad oil, mustard, or vinegar. Pickles, rolls of herring, or white cheese also can be served with the eggs.

Manfred Ketschker
Halle-Saale, Germany

WINE CREAM

1/2 quart (2 cups) white wine

Juice and grated peel of 1 lemon

6 egg yolks

6 tablespoons sugar

1 package (1/4 ounce) unflavored gelatin

1 pint whipping cream, whipped

Maraschino cherries and grapes to garnish

Combine wine, lemon juice and peel, egg yolks, and sugar in the top of a double-boiler and beat over boiling water until foamy and like a soft custard. Dissolve gelatin in water, as directed on the package, and mix into the egg cream. Refrigerate, stirring several times. When the mixture begins to set, fold in the whipped cream. To serve, place in dessert glasses and decorate with cherries and grapes.

Clara Diedrich
Klein Winterheim, Germany

REPUBLIC OF GEORGIA

3rd Week of October
TBILISOBA FESTIVAL

On the Sunday closest to October 20, families from around the Republic of Georgia come to the capital city of Tbilisi for a harvest festival they call Tbilisoba. They join those living in the city for a day of celebration and merrymaking which has been the focus of thanksgiving for a good harvest for many centuries.

The villagers build huts in the center of the city which resemble the ones at home; inside they offer for sale the fresh products and crafts of their region. Long lines are usual as people vie for handwoven carpets, traditional Georgian dresses from the Caucasus, jewelry, crockery, and other handmade articles which clearly identify their home area and traditions.

Candies called Churchkhela and newly harvested Georgian wines are especially popular, as is cheese bread known as Khachapuri. Khachapuri is always present at dining tables in this republic, whose fertile soil has attracted invasions of Persians, Romans, Arabs, Turks, and Mongols in ages past.

In the restored old city, entertainment includes poetry-reading, folk dancing, comedy acts, and soul-searching dramas. At the end of a busy growing season, it is good to relax, to eat favorite foods, and to celebrate.

CHICKEN WITH AJICA SAUCE

1 small chicken
Ajica Sauce
Cooking oil

Clean and dry the chicken and brush Ajica Sauce over it and inside the cavity. Heat cooking oil in a frying pan, add the chicken, cover, and simmer for 30 minutes or until tender. When almost fully cooked, uncover and allow the chicken to become crisp and a reddish brown color by turning on all sides. If necessary, baste with more sauce; serve sauce on the side.

AJICA SAUCE

2 pounds dried red hot peppers, ground
4 garlic bulbs, ground
2 bunches fresh cilantro, ground
Salt to taste
2 teaspoons dry coriander
1 teaspoon saffron
1 cup finely ground walnuts
1 teaspoon oriental spice (optional)

Combine the ingredients, mix well and put in airtight covered containers. Ajica Sauce may be kept at room temperature. Use as a spicy condiment with any meal.

Eliso Frutiger
Tbilisi, Georgia

KHACHAPURI
(Georgian Cheese Bread)

DOUGH
3 cups all-purpose flour
1 teaspoon baking soda
8 tablespoons (1/2 cup) butter or margarine
8 ounces yogurt

1 pound mozzarella cheese, shredded
1/2 pound feta cheese, crumbled
1 egg (or egg substitute)

Make dough by mixing flour, baking soda, and butter together by hand; add yogurt. Put in a warm place for 10 to 15 minutes. Mix cheeses with the egg. Divide both dough and cheese mixtures into 4 equal parts. Work separately with each part.

Flatten the first piece of dough until it is 6 inches across and thick enough that the cheese filling will not break through. Place one part of the cheese mixture on the dough. Close dough around the cheese by pulling edges together over the center. Press with the thumb to seal. Set aside for 15 minutes. Then place dough, seam-side down, in a hot greased pan 7 or 8 inches in diameter and carefully flatten with the hand so that the cheese bread fills the pan. Cook for 3 or 4 minutes, flip over, and fry the second side. Continue with the other 3 parts. Butter tops and serve hot. Serves 4.

Ketevan Mennenoh
Tbilisi and Atlanta, Georgia

minutes or more, without adding flour, until the dough becomes dry and hard so that the khinkali will not fall apart when they are boiled.

Cut dough into 4 pieces. Roll each piece into a thin layer about 1/4-inch high and cut into 10 rounds each about 3 inches in diameter. Roll out each round on a well-floured surface to 6 or 7 inches. Place a teaspoon or more of the meat mixture in the center and collect edges together to form a wrinkled pouch. Twist together at the top and press lightly to seal; do the same for all rounds. Fill a medium-size saucepan 2/3 full with water and add 2 teaspoons salt or more, pepper, and 1 or 2 bay leaves. Bring to a boil. Reduce heat, carefully add 8 to 10 khinkalis and cook until they float, about 15 minutes. Repeat until all are cooked. Makes about 50 khinkalis and serves 6 to 8.

George Gogishvili
Tbilisi and Atlanta, Georgia

KHINKALI
(Meat Dumplings)

2/3 pound ground beef or mutton
1/3 pound ground pork
Salt and pepper to taste
3 small onions, finely chopped
1/2 cup water
5 cups flour
1 cup warm water
1 egg

Mix any combination of ground meat with salt, pepper, and onions. Add 1/2 cup water and mix well. Put flour in a larger bowl, make a hole in the center and fill with 1 cup warm water and the egg. Mix well and place on a floured board. Knead by hand for 15

BAJA
(Walnut Sauce)

1/2 to 1 cup of finely ground walnuts
3 or 4 cloves of garlic, ground
1 teaspoon saffron
1 teaspoon dried coriander
3 sprigs fresh cilantro
2 or 3 teaspoons vinegar
Salt and pepper to taste
Chicken broth

Mix the first 7 ingredients, adding only enough broth to make a smooth sauce that is not too thin. Serve cold. Baja is always present on a Georgian table and makes an excellent sauce for roast chicken.

TURKEY

4th Week of October
REPUBLIC DAY

In October of 1923, a new republic was established in Turkey, the link between Europe and Asia which had been ruled by the Ottoman Empire for 600 years. Each year on October 29, Republic Day celebrates that sovereignty and also honors the man who made it possible, Mustafa Kemal. Known as Atatürk, this "Father of the Turks" established an army and led the fight for independence against Ottoman traditions and World War I occupying forces.

Atatürk's visions for the new nation offered a sharp contrast to the Ottoman dynasty. The first Islamic nation to become a republic, Turkey led the way with dramatic modernization, social changes, and economic stability still in force today.

Republic Day begins with a respectful ceremony in the capital, Ankara, at the grand mausoleum of Atatürk, who died in 1938. Parades and torch-lit processions take place in every city, fireworks explode throughout the nation, and in the evening formal balls and exhibitions of folk dancing are held.

Turkey also celebrates children with an international festival in Ankara in April and Youth and Sports Day in May. Every month there is a festival somewhere in Thrace, the European end of the country, or in Anatolia (Asia Minor).

Seventy centuries of the lavish living of the sultans fed into Turkish cuisine — most famous for Shish Kebab, skewered mutton and vegetables, and thick and sweet Turkish coffee. Also tempting are Dolmas, grape leaves stuffed with beef, and Ic Pilavi, a special rice cooked with currants, pine nuts, chopped liver, and spices. The national drink of anisette, called *raki*, is usually served with a variety of *meze* (hors d'oeuvres).

Gülten Erkan prepares to make Zucchini Patties in her kitchen.

PATLECAN KEBAB
(Eggplant Kebab)

1/2 pound ribeye beef steak, cubed

Corn oil

1 small onion, diced

1 medium tomato, chopped

1 bell pepper, divided

Salt and pepper to taste

2 eggplants

4 cherry tomatoes

1 tablespoon tomato paste

Sauté meat in a frying pan in a little oil and add onions, then chopped tomato. Cut four squares of bell pepper and set aside; dice the remainder and add to the pan. Add salt and pepper and cook over low heat for a few minutes. When meat is tender, remove the mixture to a bowl.

Make "pajama stripes" on the eggplant by peeling off narrow strips of the purple skin; then cut each eggplant into 4 lengthwise strips 1/4 inch thick. Lightly fry in hot oil and drain on paper towels.

Prepare kebabs: Overlap ends of 2 eggplant strips (see photo p. 130), place 2 tablespoons of meat mixture at the center, and fold eggplant toward the center to enclose the meat. Add a pepper square and a cherry tomato on top and anchor with a toothpick. Arrange in a casserole. Blend a little water into the tomato paste and pour over the kebabs. Bake for 45 minutes at 350° F and serve hot with fluffy white rice. Serves 4.

Gülten Erkan
Ankara, Turkey, and Atlanta, Georgia

MUJVER
(Zucchini Patties)

2 pounds zucchini
1 teaspoon salt
6 eggs
5 heaping tablespoons flour
1/2 bunch fresh mint, chopped (or 1 tablespoon dried)
1/2 bunch green onions, finely chopped
1/2 bunch fresh dill, chopped (or 1 tablespoon dried)
1/4 pound feta cheese, crumbled
1 teaspoon black pepper
1 cup peanut oil

Grate zucchini. Place in a large bowl, add salt, and let stand for at least 1 hour. Put in a strainer and

press with the palm to drain juice. Squeeze again by hand until the juice is completely removed. In a bowl, combine zucchini and remaining ingredients except oil. Mix well with a wooden spoon.

Heat peanut oil in a nonstick pan over medium heat. When the oil becomes very hot, add serving spoonfuls of the mixture, pressing each patty with the back of the spoon to flatten. Fry each side until golden. Drain on a paper towel. If needed, add more oil and reheat before adding more mixture. Serve hot or warm.

Gülten Erkan

REVANI
(A Syrup Cake)

SYRUP

1 cup sugar
2 cups water
4 tablespoons (1/4 cup) unsalted butter
Juice of 1/2 lemon

6 eggs
1 1/4 cups sugar
1 1/4 cups cream of wheat
1/4 cup flour
1 tablespoon grated lemon peel
Whipped cream, sweetened
Chopped walnuts

Make a light syrup: combine sugar, water, and butter and boil for about 20 minutes; add lemon juice and boil for another 10 to 15 minutes. Set aside to cool.

Beat eggs and sugar until thick and fluffy. Add cream of wheat, flour, and lemon peel; mix well. Pour into a bundt pan or a 9″ x 13″ glass cake pan, lightly covered with cooking spray. Bake in a preheated 350° F oven for 40 to 50 minutes, or until a toothpick inserted in the center comes out clean.

Remove from the oven, make several holes in the top with the point of a knife, and pour the cooled syrup over the cake. (Remove from a bundt pan when slightly cooled by inverting onto a cake plate.) To serve, slice and top with sweetened whipped cream and a sprinkle of chopped walnuts. Serves 12.

Ferhan Sahinci
Izmir, Turkey

MIDYE DOLMASI
(Stuffed Mussels)

30 to 35 mussels
1/2 cup olive oil
4 large onions, finely chopped
1/4 cup pine nuts
3/4 cup rice
1/3 cup currants, soaked in warm water
1 tablespoon sugar
1/4 cup finely chopped fresh dill (or 2 tablespoons
    dried)
2 tablespoons chopped parsley
2 tablespoons dried mint
1/4 teaspoon salt
1 teaspoon black pepper
1/2 teaspoon allspice
1/2 cup hot water
Lemon halves

Mussels must be closed. Scrub with a stiff brush under cold running water. Remove beards and soak mussels in cold water for 60 minutes, changing water every 20 minutes to remove sand. Place in a large skillet with only water clinging to the shells. Cover and cook over high heat for about 2 minutes, shaking the skillet occasionally until the shells open.

Discard those which do not. Strain liquid through several layers of cheesecloth and reserve.

Heat oil in the skillet and sauté onions until golden. Add pine nuts and sauté for 2 minutes. Add rice and sauté for 1 minute. Add currants, sugar, herbs, and spices, mixing well. Add 1/2 cup of the mussel broth and hot water. Bring to a boil, mixing constantly. Lower heat and simmer for 10 minutes. Remove from heat and let cool. Open mussels slightly with an oyster knife and stuff each with a little rice mixture. Close and tie mussels with string. Place in a heavy pan, add boiling water to barely cover, and simmer for 15 minutes. Remove mussels with a slotted spoon and cool to room temperature. Remove strings and serve with lemon halves. Serves 4.

Gülten Erkan

Fried eggplant slices enclose a meat filling, and a pepper square and salad tomato add color to the top of Eggplant Kebabs.

England: Shirley Brown with her English Trifle

SOUTHEASTERN STATES, U.S.A.

1st Week of November
TAILGATING

Tailgatin'! In the Southeast this unique tradition manifests itself throughout the fall months when football reigns supreme . . . during holiday weekends in the long hot summers when outdoor concerts draw large crowds . . . and at steeplechasing events in both spring and fall. From a picnic in the stadium parking lot, to full meals at a concert site or in a steeplechase meadow, the food gets progressively more elegant and tailgating is an exciting phenomenon.

—TAILGATE PARTIES—

Football fever passes through the South like a plague from late August to the bowl games that end the year. Two great gridiron conferences with tough schedules — the Southeastern (SEC) and the Atlantic Coast (ACC) — keep enthusiasts close to the stadium or the television. Football rivalries seem to be more serious here, with families often divided in loyalty — for Georgia Tech fans, for instance, denigration of the University of Georgia Bulldogs is considered a birthright — the "Ramblin' Wreck" fight song lays down the rules.

Tailgating is one way to raise enthusiasm for the team. Coming early to the stadium parking lot to eat "vittles" off the back "gate" of a station wagon or van stirs up the blood in anticipation. After the game, the spread allows great rejoicing for the winning team's fans, joint commiseration and laying of blame for those who lost.

Oh, to be in the Southland in early November when cool air has finally arrived, football teams are ripe, the portable grill is smokin', and tailgatin' is the favored way to take in nourishment!

TAILGATIN' HAMBURGERS

1.

Mix 1 pound lean ground beef with finely chopped onion and pieces of bleu cheese to taste. Grill as desired.

2.

To 1 1/2 pounds ground beef (chuck) add a small chopped onion, 1/4 cup ketchup, 1 teaspoon mustard, salt and pepper, and enough bread crumbs to hold the burgers together. Take care not to burn while grilling.

BIG ORANGE DATE CAKE

1 cup butter

2 cups sugar

4 eggs

4 cups flour (reserve 1/2 cup)

1/4 teaspoon salt

1 1/2 teaspoon baking soda

2/3 cup orange juice

2/3 cup buttermilk

8 ounces dates, chopped

1 cup chopped pecans

1 teaspoon vanilla

4 tablespoons orange rind

FROSTING

1/2 cup orange juice

2 cups powdered sugar

4 tablespoons orange rind

Grease and flour a 10-inch bundt pan. Beat butter and sugar until light and fluffy. Add eggs one at a time. Mix 3 1/2 cups flour, salt, and soda and add to the mixture. Beat in orange juice and buttermilk. Dredge dates and pecans in the reserved flour and fold into the batter. Stir in vanilla and orange rind. Bake for 60 to 75 minutes in a preheated 350° F oven. Cool in the pan for 15 minutes.

To make frosting, combine ingredients and drizzle over the cake. Serves 15–20.

Betty Rose
Knoxville, Tennessee

FRESH FRUIT CUP

Prepare bite-size pieces of firm fresh fruit of choice: bananas, pears, apples, plums, mangoes, and

The grill is set on a folding table in the stadium parking lot, and the hamburgers, Freezer Cole Slaw, Fresh Fruit Cup, and Big Orange Date Cake are ready.

pineapple. Place fruit in a plastic container with a tight lid. Cover fruit completely with orange juice until it overflows when the lid is snapped into place, forcing air out. Keep on ice or refrigerate. Do not open until ready to eat. Remove fruit with a slotted spoon; orange juice may then be served as a fruit punch. May be prepared a day ahead.

Beth Gramling
Orangeburg, South Carolina

FREEZER COLE SLAW

1 medium cabbage, shredded
1 teaspoon salt
2 carrots, shredded
1 green pepper, chopped

DRESSING
1 cup vinegar
1/4 cup water
1 teaspoon mustard seed
1 teaspoon celery seed
2 cups sugar

Shred cabbage, drain, and add salt. Mix and let stand for 1 hour. Squeeze out excess moisture and add carrots and green pepper. Combine the dressing ingredients and boil for 1 minute. Cool to lukewarm and pour over the slaw mixture. Put in a container and freeze. Take the slaw frozen to the picnic or set out for an hour to thaw. Leftover slaw can be refrozen, even more than once, and will retain quality for a long time.

Betty Donato
Peachtree City, Georgia

—POPS IN THE PARK—

On a checkered picnic cloth sprawled on a hillside . . . arranged on folding tables at a lakeside amphitheater . . . or grouped seductively at a parkland concert site — picnic fare seems to taste better with music in the background. On festive holiday weekends like July 4th and Labor Day, dining to music adds a gaiety that leads naturally into the flags, fervor, and fireworks that follow the national march, "Stars and Stripes Forever." Laser shows, country artists, "pops" programs, Shakespeare festivals, opera in the park, and patriotic, jazz, and philharmonic music all lend themselves to a picnic beforehand as aficionados gather early for the best spots.

Adding to the ambience of theater under the stars are linen-set tables, folding and lounge chairs, cushions and rugs for the ground, candles and disposable containers. The menu is always a challenge to providers who strive to coordinate hot and cold foods with the right time, place, and temperature. Basically, concert dining means a bottle or two of sparkle, something tasty to go with it, and a few sprightly tunes to wash it down.

PEACH CHAMPAGNE SOUP

4 cups ripe peaches, peeled and sliced
1/3 cup sugar
3/4 teaspoon almond extract
Grated rind and juice of 1 orange
2 cups champagne, chilled
Garnish: orange peel twists

Purée peaches and sugar in a blender. Pour into a mixing bowl and add almond extract, orange rind, and juice. Chill. When ready to serve, slowly stir in champagne. Spoon into bowls and serve immediately, garnished with orange peel twists. Or transport to the concert site in an air-tight container. Serves 6.

Note: Adding more champagne will change this recipe from soup to a delicious drink. The mixture will keep, although its peachy color darkens the day after it is made.

Betty Donato
Peachtree City, Georgia

GRANDMA'S YEAST ROLLS

1 pint (2 cups) sweet milk
2 tablespoons butter
2 tablespoons sugar
1 teaspoon salt
1 yeast cake (or 2 packets dry yeast)
1/4 cup lukewarm water
3 cups flour or more, as needed

Scald milk and pour over the butter, sugar, and salt. Cool. Dissolve the yeast cake in water and stir into the mixture. Add flour, beat well, and let rise in a warm place. Then add enough extra flour to knead thoroughly. Allow to rise again until light. Shape into rolls and let rise again. Bake in a preheated 400° F oven until lightly browned. For a concert spread, cut rolls in half and serve with slices of thin ham.

Mary Alice Blanton
Louisville, Kentucky

PASTA PRIMAVERA

8 tablespoons (1/2 cup) unsalted butter
1 medium onion, minced
1 teaspoon minced garlic
1 pound fresh asparagus, trimmed and cut diagonally
* into 1/4-inch slices, or frozen asparagus*
1 medium zucchini, cut into 1/4-inch-thick rounds

1 small carrot, cut into wafer-thin slices

1/2 pound mushrooms, sliced

1 cup whipping cream

1/3 cup chicken stock

2 tablespoons chopped fresh basil (1 teaspoon dried)

1 cup frozen peas, thawed

2 ounces prosciutto ham, chopped

3 green onions, chopped

Salt and freshly ground pepper, to taste

1 pound fettuccine or spaghetti, cooked and drained

1 cup freshly grated Parmesan cheese

1/3 cup pine nuts, toasted

Elegance makes the difference between a steeplechase "spread" and tailgating at a sports event.

In a large skillet over medium heat, sauté onion and garlic in butter until softened, about 2 minutes. Add asparagus, zucchini, carrots, and mushrooms; stir fry for 2 minutes. Increase heat to high and add cream, chicken stock, and basil. Boil for about 3 minutes, until liquid is slightly reduced. Stir in peas, ham, and green onions; simmer for 1 minute. Add salt and pepper, drained pasta, cheese, and pine nuts, tossing until thoroughly mixed. Turn onto a warmed platter and serve with crusty French bread or yeast rolls. To take to a concert site, do not chill; keep warm and serve in a chafing dish over a candle.

Mary Kitchens
Atlanta, Georgia

CHOCOLATE CARAMEL BARS

1 package (14 ounces) caramels

1 can (5 ounces) evaporated milk, divided

German chocolate cake mix with pudding (18 ounces)

12 tablespoons (3/4 cup) butter or margarine, melted

1 egg

6 ounces semisweet chocolate morsels

1 cup coarsely chopped pecans

Combine caramels and 1/4 cup evaporated milk in a small saucepan. Cook over low heat, stirring occasionally until smooth; set aside. Combine cake mix, butter, egg, and remaining evaporated milk. Spoon half of the mixture into a greased 9″ x 13″ pan, spreading evenly. Bake for 6 minutes at 350° F. Remove from the oven; sprinkle with morsels and pecans. Spoon caramel mixture on top and carefully add remaining cake mixture over the caramel layer. Continue to bake for 20 to 25 minutes at 350° F. Cool on a wire rack and cut into bars. Yields about 3 dozen.

Geneva Madden
Louisville, Kentucky

—DINING AT THE RACE—

Steeplechasing is an exciting part of thoroughbred racing which combines the speed of the flat track, the thrill of a cross-country hunt, and the excitement of highly trained horses prevailing over obstacles. Outdoor dining at a steeplechase event — amid the splendors of spring or in the sparkling air of autumn — combines the plebeian picnic with the elegance of formal dining.

County Cork in Ireland claims the first steeplechase in 1752 — some say the horses raced from one village church steeple to the next. It took hold in England, home of the Grand National since 1839, and crossed to America in that same decade. The southeastern states of Kentucky, Tennessee, Georgia, the Carolinas, and Virginia are especially suited for spring and fall steeplechasing they host 17 of 24 spring races and 9 of 16 in the fall — before as many as 18,000 spectators.

Many of those come early to set up tent parties or folding buffet tables near the brush jumps on a farm meadow or race track. Fancy linens, candelabra, china, crystal, and abundant flowers dazzle judges during the competition for tailgate creativity and style. Infield activities range from art markets to musical entertainment; the "mode du jour" ranges from bright-colored jackets and designer outfits to blue jeans.

Before race stewards in smart hunting jackets, jodhpurs, and caps call "post time" at 1:00 P.M., the elegant outdoor cocktail party has gone through appetizers such as crabmeat biscuits and entrées like Salmon Mousse or Veal and Ham Pie. Champagne toasts are raised for each winning jockey, and bounteous snacks sustain the crowd through the afternoon race card — a superbly elegant way to enjoy the "Sport of Kings"!

CHILLED RATATOUILLE

1/4 cup salad or olive oil
2 cloves garlic, minced
1 onion, sliced
1 green pepper, seeded and cut into strips
3 medium zucchini, cut into 1/4-inch slices
1 medium eggplant, pared and cubed
1 1/2 teaspoon salt
Seasonings:
2 teaspoons basil
1 teaspoon oregano
1/8 teaspoon black pepper
4 tomatoes, peeled and cut into wedges

In a large skillet, heat oil and add garlic, onion, green pepper, and zucchini. Cook and stir for about 3 minutes, until onion is tender. Add eggplant, salt, and seasonings, cover, and cook over medium heat for 15 minutes, stirring occasionally. Add tomatoes, cover, and cook until tomatoes are heated. Refrigerate for several hours or overnight. Serves 6 to 8.

Betty Donato
Peachtree City, Georgia

VEAL AND HAM PIE

PASTRY
1/2 cup plus 1 tablespoon boiling water
1 cup lard
3 cups flour
3/4 teaspoon salt

FILLING
1 pound boneless smoked ham, cubed
3 shallots, minced
2 tablespoons butter
1 tablespoon Madeira wine
1 1/2 pounds boneless veal, cubed
1/3 cup brandy
1/3 cup chicken broth
1/4 cup chopped fresh parsley
2 tablespoons lemon juice
1 tablespoon grated lemon peel

SEASONINGS

Salt to taste

1/2 teaspoon marjoram

1/4 teaspoon each: tarragon and white pepper

A pinch of thyme

4 hard-boiled eggs

1 tablespoon whipping cream

1 envelope unflavored gelatin

1 cup chicken broth

To make the pastry: Pour boiling water over lard and refrigerate for 15 minutes. Mix flour and salt; add to the lard and stir with a fork until the mixture clings together. Shape into a ball and refrigerate for 30 minutes. Roll 2/3 of the dough into a 13″ x 8″ rectangle. Carefully place into a 9″ x 5″ x 3″ greased loaf pan and press to fit. Trim edges, leaving 1/4-inch overhang.

To prepare filling: Sauté ham and shallots in butter and wine over high heat for 5 minutes. Remove and add next 6 ingredients and the seasonings. Mix well and spread half over the pastry. Place whole eggs in a row down the center. Top with other half of the mixture. Roll out remaining dough, place over the meat, and top with decorative cutouts from the scraps. Brush dough and cutouts with cream.

Place the loaf pan on an ovenproof sheet and bake for 15 minutes at 425° F. Reduce heat to 350° F and bake for 45 minutes. Then reduce heat to 325° F and bake for 60 minutes. Cool for 30 minutes. Soften gelatin by heating in 1 cup chicken broth. Make a small hole in the pie, insert a funnel and pour in broth 2 tablespoons at a time. Tilt gently so broth is distributed evenly. Cool, then refrigerate for 4 hours or overnight. Slice and serve with Mustard Sauce. As an entrée, serves 6.

MUSTARD SAUCE

2 tablespoons dry mustard

2 teaspoons warm water

1/4 cup vinegar

1 cup sour cream

1 tablespoon Worcestershire sauce

Salt and pepper to taste

Mix dry mustard, warm water, and vinegar. Whisk in sour cream, Worcestershire, and salt and pepper to taste.

Mary Kitchens
Atlanta, Georgia

CHOCOLATE CHIP PIE

1 cup sugar

1/4 cup cornstarch

2 eggs, beaten

8 tablespoons (1/2 cup) butter, melted

2 tablespoons bourbon

1 cup finely chopped pecans

6 ounces chocolate chips

1 unbaked 9-inch pie shell

Bourbon

Dairy topping or whipped cream

Heat oven to 350° F. In a small bowl, combine sugar and cornstarch. Stir in beaten eggs and add butter, bourbon, pecans, and chips. Blend and pour into the pie shell. Bake for 45 to 50 minutes.

Cool for 1 hour and add bourbon-flavored topping: Mix 1 cup thawed dairy topping with 1 tablespoon or more bourbon until well blended. Or add 1 to 2 teaspoons bourbon to lightly sweetened whipped cream.

Mary Alice Blanton
Louisville, Kentucky

AUSTRIA

2nd Week of November
ST. MARTIN'S DAY

For Austrians, the focus of St. Martin's Day on November 11 is split between celebration of the patron saint of Burgenland and the end of the wine growers' year. Many cities and villages hold official feasts in honor of both.

The traditional food of the day is roast goose, or Martinigansl. According to common legend, when St. Martin was called to become Bishop of Tours, France, in the year 371, he hid himself in a stable to avoid the appointment. He was betrayed by a goose whose loud honking revealed the hiding place. Born in Hungary, Martin entered military service at age 15 but, after a vision of Jesus, became a Christian and pacifist.

The new wine competes with Martin and his goose. Austria is a land of vineyards, and wine "baptisms" — known as Martin's Praise — are held in many locales. Wine restaurants known as Heurigen are common in grape-growing districts and attract as many patrons as Viennese coffee-houses.

Austrians also gather at three other institutions unique to their country: the Kaffeehaus, Konditorei, and Beisel. The Koffeehaus goes back to 1683, when a retreating Turkish army left behind its store of coffee beans; it is said that Vienna alone has more than 2,000 coffeehouses. The Konditorei is the renowned Viennese pastry shop — a place to sit, share a chat, and forget calories — while the Beisel is a blue-collar corner pub.

The Heuriger is an indoor tavern with an out-door garden, where the vintner sells his own wine and a few items of simple food to a mingling of social classes and ages. What better way is there to spend Martini-Tag on a crisp autumn evening?

A beautiful roast goose is the only entrée considered on Martini-Tag in Austria.

MARTINIGANSL

(Roast Goose)

8- to 10-pound goose
Salt and marjoram to taste
1 small apple, cored but not peeled
1 teaspoon flour
Butter, melted, as needed

Clean and wash the goose. Sprinkle with salt on the outside; rub marjoram on the inside. Fill the cavity with the whole cored apple. Place the goose in a roasting pan, add an inch or more of water, and bake for 2 1/2 to 3 hours in a preheated 325° F oven. Baste frequently with drippings and turn the bird once halfway through the baking time. Make gravy by thickening the juices with a mixture of flour and melted butter. Serves 6 to 8.

Serve with any combination of dumplings, rice, red or wine cabbage, chestnuts, or a salad.

Gertraud Lebisch
Vienna, Austria

SEMMELKNÖDEL
(Dumplings)

8 slices white bread, cubed
1/2 medium onion, chopped
Chopped parsley
6 tablespoons margarine
2 eggs, beaten
1 cup milk
Salt
2 tablespoons flour

Lightly fry the bread, onion, and parsley in margarine. Pour beaten eggs and milk over the bread cubes (the amount of milk depends on dryness of the bread). Add salt and allow the mass to rest for 20 minutes. Then stir in enough flour to form round dumplings which are firm enough to keep their shape — a trifle smaller than tennis balls. Simmer in boiling water for 10 to 15 minutes; dumplings are done when they rise to the surface. Makes 6.

Rudolph Eigner
Krems, Austria

CHRISTA'S WACHAUER TORTE

7 eggs, separated
1 scant cup (5 ounces) sugar
3 1/2 ounces dark chocolate
5 ounces almonds, ground

FILLING
1/2 cup sugar
7 tablespoons butter
3 1/2 ounces chocolate, melted
1 egg plus 1 egg yolk
Apricot jam

Separate the eggs. Beat egg whites to stiff peaks, slowly adding half the sugar. Set aside. In a mixer, beat the yolks well, add remaining sugar, and continue beating for 5 minutes. While preheating the oven to 300° to 350° F, place chocolate in a metal container on the oven shelf to melt. Add the almonds and melted chocolate to the yolk mixture and stir well. Carefully fold in the beaten egg whites. Pour into a buttered and floured 9-inch cake pan. Bake until a toothpick or needle inserted in the center comes out clean. Set aside to cool completely.

For the filling, cream sugar and butter until smooth and light colored. Slowly add melted chocolate, egg, and the extra yolk. Slice the cooled cake into 3 layers and add filling between the layers. Smooth the top of the torte with a thin layer of warmed apricot jam and add glaze — a mixture of melted sweet dark chocolate and butter.

Christa Heisler
Krems, Austria

ENGLAND

3rd Week of November
SUNDAY DINNER WITH THE FAMILY

Since members of English families may live many miles from their roots, coming back home for dinner after church on Sunday is a joyous occasion for catching up on news of each other and partaking of what might be called England's national dish, Roast Beef and Yorkshire Puddings. For farm families, the beef might come from their own stock, selected by the menfolk, killed humanely, and dressed by the local butcher.

Through the centuries, the English mother or "Mum" has been the driving force behind keeping the family unit intact or gathering them back for one more Sunday lunch together. She cooks her family's favorites, dresses the table with a blooming plant or a bunch of field flowers in a jug, perhaps a gift from a family member. Beef is the usual hearty favorite; the accompanying vegetables include runner beans, minted peas, carrots and sweet, yellow turnips — mostly steamed — and, if not Yorkshire Puddings, then mashed potatoes.

The holidays most observed by English families are the religious ones, along with May Day, Boxing Day, and Guy Fawkes Day on November 5, also known as Bonfire Day. Fireworks and beacon lights illuminate England from one end to the other, even today an act of thanksgiving for the failure of a treasonous plot in 1605.

Among the most ancient celebrations are Harvest Festivals held in most parish churches each fall and especially beloved by schoolchildren, who often fill boxes of food and take handmade items to church to be blessed before the gifts are carried off to a charitable home or hospital. In former times, the last sheath ceremoniously cut by the reapers was hung in the village church in thanksgiving for the good harvest. The children's gift-giving today is a continuation of that custom.

In a newer custom on the Sunday after Christmas, Councilwoman Theresa Russell of Newcastle-upon-Tyne provides Roast Beef and Yorkshire Puddings for an international gathering — and invites Christians, Muslims, Hindus, Jews, Mohammedans and Sikhs, in effect a microcosm of the whole-world family.

ROAST BEEF AND YORKSHIRE PUDDINGS

Allow 8 ounces per person of any cut of roasting beef. Brush beef with oil and sprinkle with salt and pepper. Place in a roasting pan in the center of a preheated hot oven (400° F). Reduce oven heat to 350°F. Allow 20 minutes per pound cooking time and an additional 20 minutes. With fat from the roasting tin, baste the joint during cooking. About 1 hour before beef is cooked, place small new potatoes around the meat. Make sure they are covered in drippings from the tin and turn occasionally. Serve with seasonal vegetables. Keep roast and potatoes warm while you make Yorkshire Puddings.

YORKSHIRE PUDDINGS
2/3 cup flour
1 medium egg
1/4 pint (1/2 cup) half milk–half water, or all water
1/4 teaspoon salt

Mix ingredients to the consistency of pancake batter, adding more water or flour as needed. Place deep bun tins (6-compartment muffin tins, 2 or 2 1/2 inches across) in the oven and add oil into the base of each, heating until very hot. Pour mixture into the tins, filling each just slightly more than halfway. Cook in a 450° F oven — on the shelf just above the center — for 15 minutes, but do not open the oven door during cooking.

While Yorkshire puddings are cooking, make gravy: Drain drippings from the roasting pan into a bowl and measure 1 1/2 pints (3 cups); if needed, add water drained from vegetables. For added flavor, dissolve 2 beef stock cubes in the drippings. Pour into a large frying pan, heat to boiling, and thicken with cornflour (cornstarch) mixed in cold water. Reduce heat and stir continuously until the gravy is smooth and bubbling.

Theresa Russell
Newcastle-upon-Tyne

CARROTS AND SWEDES

Cook carrots and Swedish turnips together in salted water. (Swedes are a sweet yellow turnip, similar to American rutabagas.) When cooked, mash with butter and fresh-ground black pepper.

To add even more color to a dinner of Roast Beef and Yorkshire Puddings, serve peas, beans, Brussels sprouts, or other green vegetables.

Frances Green
Botley, England

OLDE ENGLISH SHERRY TRIFLE

1 small sponge or angel food cake, cut or broken in pieces
6 tablespoons sweet sherry
1 large can (29 ounces) peaches
1 small package (3 ounces) custard (vanilla pudding)
1 3-ounce packet raspberry or apricot gelatin
1/2 pint whipping cream, sweetened with sugar if desired
Chopped nuts or chocolate shavings to decorate (optional)

Cover the bottom of an 8-inch glass bowl with cake pieces and soak with sherry. Cover with peaches or any fruit preference and soak with a little juice. Make custard pudding and cover the fruit. Make gelatin and add on top of the pudding. Refrigerate overnight. When ready to serve, beat cream until stiff, add sugar, and mound on top. If desired, sprinkle with nuts and chocolate.

Shirley Brown
Hart Village, Cleveland, England

PEPPER STEAKS

6 sirloin steaks
Peppercorns, crushed
Salt to taste
4 tablespoons (1/4 cup) butter
2 onions, chopped finely
6 mushrooms, chopped finely
4 cloves garlic, chopped
1 teaspoon English mustard
2 tablespoons Worcestershire sauce
6 drops Tabasco sauce
2 tablespoons brandy
Double (heavy) cream

Cover one side of the steaks with peppercorns; sprinkle the other with salt. Place onions, mushrooms, and garlic in a large saucepan over low heat and sauté slowly in butter until golden. Add mustard, Worcestershire, and Tabasco. Place steaks on top of the sautéed mixture, peppercorn side up, cover and cook slowly. When almost done, add brandy and enough double cream to make a thicker sauce. Serves 6.

Frances Green

NEW ENGLAND STATES, U.S.A.

4th Week of November
THANKSGIVING DAY

Plymouth, Massachusetts, December 1621. After months of almost unbearable hardships, Governor William Bradford announces that three days are to be spent in rejoicing for the survival of his small community of Pilgrims. With great forethought, he invites Chief Massasoit and his 90 braves to join the settlers. It is said that, returning on the second day, the Indians brought five deer as their contribution. The tradition of gathering the family for a Thanksgiving feast had begun — as had the concept of the potluck dinner.

The potential nation organized, spread from coast to coast and even beyond, and grew in diversity. Through the centuries, however, the custom of giving thanks for a bountiful harvest and a good system of democracy remained constant, as it does today on each fourth Thursday of November.

Whether the traditional meal remained as constant is not clear. Although it is easy to picture turkeys stuffed with dressing, cranberries, and pumpkin pie at the first feast, it was more likely venison or other game. Held in New England or not, Americans tend to think of the first Thanksgiving taking place close to Plymouth Rock.

George Washington advocated Thanksgiving Day in 1789, but it was not until November 26, 1865, that President Andrew Johnson proposed a nationwide observance. Still unofficial, each year the president must proclaim it anew, perhaps as a sign that the nation's blessings should not be taken for granted.

ROAST TURKEY WITH CHESTNUT STUFFING

10- to 16-pound turkey
1/2 cup each chopped onion and celery
4 tablespoons (1/4 cup) butter or margarine
1 tablespoon dried parsley flakes
1 1/2 teaspoons thyme leaf, crumbled
1 teaspoon salt
1/2 teaspoon pepper
1 cup canned chestnuts, chopped
1/3 cup water
6 slices white bread, toasted and cubed
Melted butter
Paprika

Rinse turkey well, rub outside with butter, and sprinkle with salt and pepper. Make the stuffing: Sauté onion and celery in butter until soft. Stir in parsley, thyme, salt, pepper, chestnuts, and water. Bring to a boil, pour over the bread cubes, and toss until moist. Place the turkey — breast up in an uncovered roasting pan. Loosely fill body and neck cavities with dressing and close with skewers. Cover with a loose tent of aluminum foil.

Roast in a preheated 450° F oven for 20 minutes; then reduce heat to 325° F and allow 18 to 25 minutes per pound. Occasionally baste with melted butter and paprika. Remove the foil tent for the last 30 minutes of cooking to allow the turkey to brown. When ready, drumsticks should move easily in their sockets, the turkey should be golden brown, and a cooking thermometer should register 180° to 185° F. Serves 12.

Sally Kuras
West Suffield, Connecticut

CRANBERRY-ORANGE RELISH

2 medium oranges
2 cups (1 pound) fresh cranberries
2 cups sugar
1/4 cup English walnuts, chopped

Scrape 1 tablespoon of peel from oranges; peel and section oranges and cut each section into several pieces. Grind cranberries. Mix all ingredients, cover, and refrigerate. May be frozen for 6 months or refrigerated for 2 weeks. As a relish, it will serve 12 to 16.

Marlene Meyer
West Des Moines, Iowa

BRUSSELS SPROUTS VERONIQUE

2 pints Brussels sprouts
1 cup celery, diced
1 1/2 cups white sauce or 1 envelope white-sauce mix
3 tablespoons mayonnaise or salad dressing
1 cup seedless green grapes, halved
1/4 cup slivered almonds, toasted and chopped

Trim Brussels sprouts and cut each in half. In a covered saucepan, cook sprouts and celery in boiling salted water for 10 minutes or until tender. Drain well, return to the pan, and set aside. Make white sauce and stir in mayonnaise or salad dressing. Pour over the sprouts and celery and heat slowly; fold in the grapes and garnish with almonds. Serves 6.

Sally Kuras

PRALINE PUMPKIN PIE

PRALINE LAYER
1 unbaked 9-inch pie shell
3 tablespoons butter or margarine
1/3 cup firmly packed brown sugar
1/3 cup chopped pecans

CUSTARD LAYER
1 cup evaporated milk
1/2 cup water
3 eggs
1 1/2 cups canned pumpkin
1/2 cup granulated sugar
1/2 cup firmly packed brown sugar
1 1/2 teaspoons pumpkin pie spice
1 teaspoon salt (or less)
1/2 cup heavy cream, sweetened and whipped

To make the praline layer: Prepare piecrust of your choice. Roll out to a 12-inch round on a lightly floured pastry board; fit into a 9-inch pie plate. Blend butter or margarine with 1/3 cup brown sugar, add pecans, and press over the bottom of the pie shell. Bake for 10 minutes at 450° F.

To make the custard layer: In a saucepan, scald evaporated milk with water. In a large bowl, beat eggs and add pumpkin, granulated sugar, 1/2 cup brown sugar, pie spice, and salt. Beat in the scalded milk mixture. Pour over praline layer in the cooled pastry shell. Bake for 50 minutes in an oven preheated to 350° F. Cool before crowning with sweetened whipped cream.

Sally Kuras

Poland: Barszcz Uszka

NETHERLANDS

1st Week of December
ST. NICHOLAS EVE

For children and adults in Holland, December 6 is a very special day — popular St. Nicholas, the original Sinterklaas which became Santa Claus in America, and his even more popular servant, Black Peter, visit schools and homes with praise for those who have been good and advice for those who have not.

Much merriment comes from the antics of St. Nicholas and his Moorish assistant. Students greet him with songs when he visits each school to give presents and sweets to younger children, and to distribute presents and rhymes made by the older children for their secret classmates.

In the evening, children solemnly place their wooden shoes before the fire, fill them with hay and carrots for old St. Nicholas' equally old and faithful horse, and put a bowl of water nearby. They listen to hear his horse clatter about the rooftop, and in the morning eagerly look to see if presents have replaced the provisions.

With the younger children abed, the fun begins for the older ones, adult family members, friends, and neighbors. Speculaas and other Christmas pastries are served with coffee and tea, chocolate milk, anise milk, or Bisschopswijn.

Pakjes prepared in secret are placed in a large basket ready to be passed out by St. Nicholas, who arrives with great fanfare, dressed in his red bishop's robe. Each gift includes a lighthearted poem meant to tease the receiver, either praise for a virtue or criticism for a vice. The gift that fits the rhyme is imaginatively wrapped or concealed. To mask the true mischief makers, St. Nicholas claims each gift is from him and is based on reports from the all-seeing Black Peter. Thank you, Sinterklaas!

Although St. Nicholas Day itself is a quiet family day, as is Christmas, the night before is a mysterious time made merry with ingenious gift making as well as the antics of the lively joker, Black Peter, who carries a gunnysack in which to carry away those who have been truly bad!

A ST. NICHOLAS SURPRISE

Typical of the teasing rhymes given to children on St. Nicholas Eve is the following:

Little Mary, listen well, St. Nicholas is not very glad.

At school your teacher is complaining — your writing is so very bad! Your letters crisscross on the paper, like a skater on the rink, Or even worse, it's like a spider crawling from a jar of ink!

The poem, written on the first page of a new exercise book with illustrations of St. Nicholas, comes with "the gift" of an embroidered handkerchief, wrapped and taped inside the back of the book.

MARY OUWEHAND
THE FRIENDSHIP FORCE OF MIDDLEBURG

---

carved wooden cookie mold with rice meal or flour. Press the dough into the mold and cut off the excess with a thin knife. Lift cookies from the molds (or turn over and lightly tap the back of the form). Place on a floured baking tin. On the middle shelf of a fairly hot oven (400° F), bake cookies for about 15 minutes, until they are a pale brown. Remove and cool.

Diny Goossens
Arnhem, Netherlands

Red-robed St. Nicholas and his assistant Black Peter are the most essential ingredients of St. Nicholas Eve gaiety.

SPECULAAS

1/2 cup soft brown sugar
1 tablespoon milk
1 1/4 cup flour
5 tablespoons butter or margarine
1/2 teaspoon ground cloves
1/2 teaspoon cinnamon
Pinch of nutmeg
Pinch of baking powder
Rice meal or flour

Dissolve the sugar in the milk. Mix all ingredients (except rice meal) and knead into a ball. Powder a

BANKETLETTERS

ALMOND PASTE
8 ounces shelled almonds, ground
1 scant cup sugar
1 egg
Grated peel of 1/2 lemon
1 drop bitter almond oil (or 1 to 2 teaspoons almond flavoring)
1 tablespoon coffee cream

PASTRY DOUGH
1 1/4 cups flour
Pinch of salt
5/8 cup (scant 11 tablespoons) cold butter
3 tablespoons cold water
1 egg, beaten

To make almond paste: Mix ground almonds with remaining ingredients. Grind the mixture twice and knead well. Place almond paste in a bowl, cover, and allow to rest in a cool place for at least 24 hours.

(Tubes of almond paste are available in American stores; use 1 tube. Any leftover paste can be refrigerated in tightly closed jam jars for 2 to 3 weeks.)

To make pastry: Sift flour and salt; add butter and cut with two knives to a crumbly mass. With a knife, stir in cold water until a ball is formed. Roll the dough on a floured surface to a thin rectangle. Fold into thirds, turn, and fold double. Repeat the rolling and folding twice more; after the third time, allow the folded dough to rest in a cool place for 30 minutes. (Ready-made frozen puff pastry also can be used.)

Form the almond paste into 2 rolls, each 10 inches long. Roll out the folded dough into another rectangular shape about 8″ x 12″ inches and cut into 2 narrow lengths. Lay an almond roll on each and fold the dough around it, firmly closing the seam with water.

Make pastry letters by shaping the bars into letters — S for St. Nicholas, for instance, or the initial of a child's name. For some letters, such as E, pieces must be stuck together with water.

Lay pastry letters or bars, seam down, on a baking tin moistened with water. Coat tops with beaten egg. Bake in a preheated 375°–400°F oven for about 25 minutes until they are a pretty brown color.

Suzette Smissaert and Coba Weezepoel
Middleburg, Holland

PEPERNOTEN
(Ginger Nuts)

2 cups self-rising flour
3/4 cup brown sugar
8 tablespoons (1/2 cup) soft butter
2 tablespoons Parliament Cake Spices
Snuff (pinch) of salt
3 tablespoons milk

Sift the flour. Add brown sugar, butter, spices, salt, and milk. Knead to a supple pastry. Form small balls the size of marbles and place on a buttered baking tray. Bake in a 300° F oven for 20 minutes, until cooked and a pretty brown color.

Banketletters and Peppernoten, along with Speculaas, are the traditional St. Nicholas Eve refreshments.

PARLIAMENT CAKE SPICES

Mix 2 tablespoons cinnamon, 2 teaspoons each ground cloves and nutmeg, and 1 teaspoon each pepper and ground aniseed. Or use pumpkin pie spice and add a pinch of aniseed.

Co Philipse
Middleburg, Netherlands

BISSCHOPSWIJN

1 lemon
1 orange
20 cloves
1 liter red wine
2 tablespoons sugar
1/2 stick cinnamon

Wash and dry the lemon and orange. Stick 10 cloves in each. Mix wine, sugar, lemon, orange, and cinnamon in a saucepan, cover, and bring to a boil. Reduce heat to low and simmer for 1 hour. Remove orange, lemon, and cinnamon stick. To serve, heat wine to boiling once more.

Diny Goossens

KENYA

2nd Week of December
JAMHURI DAY

The political freedom attained by Kenya in 1963 after 70 years of British rule brings Kenyans together to celebrate their families as well as their country's independence.

On December 12, Nairobi city dwellers and Masai nomadic herdsmen glorify their republic, as do farmers and fishermen — suppliers of the staple foods of wheat, rice, maize, and fish. All activities are suspended as members of extended families gather in their rural ancestral houses, converging from all parts of this equatorial nation of diverse climates, occupations, and cultures.

Parents, children, aunts and uncles, and cousins — each bringing food to share — join in the family's Jamhuri Day traditions, gifting each other with chickens, local beers, or baskets of oranges, papayas, bananas, or mangoes. Although each community has a distinct way of celebrating Jamhuri, in all eight provinces the president's speech is read and the popular activities are parades and soccer games.

Other family-oriented holidays are Kenyatta Day, a political holiday which commemorates the detention of the first Kenyan president on October 20, 1952, and his release ten years later, and the usual holy days of Christians, Muslims, and Hindus. Those of the widespread Anglican faith especially believe in sharing and eating together, likening it to Jesus and His disciples. They make sure that food is bounteous, often heaping it on one platter to indicate the equality of humanity, and that enough is prepared for all possible visitors.

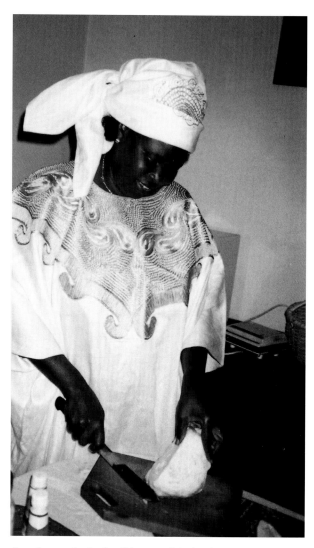

Jane Ogwayo begins her fish casserole in her home in Nairobi.

FISH CASSEROLE

Jane Ogwayo's casserole is an urban version of a traditional dish from the Lake Victoria region where fish are plentiful and potatoes grow well. Tilapia is a delicate lake fish in comparison to the much larger Nile perch.

*2 pounds of fish fillets — Tilapia, Nile Perch, or other
   lake fish*

Juice of 1 lemon

Salt to taste

Fish seasoning, garlic or curry to taste

2 cups flour

2 eggs, beaten

Bread crumbs

1 cup oil

2 or 3 potatoes, sliced

1/4 of a cabbage or 1 leek, chopped

3/4 cup water

1 chicken bouillon (or stock) cube

Thoroughly clean fish fillets and soak in lemon juice. Mix salt, seasonings, and flour and set aside 2 tablespoons. Cut fish into cubes or pieces and rub in remaining flour mixture. Dip each piece into beaten egg, roll in bread crumbs, and fry in oil until golden brown.

Peel potatoes and cut into thick slices. Boil in salted water until almost cooked. Drain and lay half of the potato slices on the bottom of a baking dish. Place fish on the top and add remaining potato slices. Cover with aluminum foil and bake for 30 to 40 minutes until tender.

Meanwhile, make a sauce by lightly frying chopped cabbage or leeks. Add a thick paste made from the reserved 2 tablespoons of seasoned flour and 3/4 cup water. Add the bouillon cube and simmer for 3 minutes. Pour over the casserole and bake for another 5 minutes, covered. Serve hot and enjoy.

Jane Ogwayo
Nairobi, Kenya

UGALI

Ugali is the most popular staple food in Kenya, especially in western Kenya where fish for dinner is popular. Maize is grown, harvested, dried, and ground into flour locally. An easy but filling dish, Ugali usually accompanies any stew or fish casserole, although boiled rice also can be served.

2 1/2 cups boiling water

2 cups maize flour (cornmeal)

8 tablespoons (1/2 cup) butter (optional)

Add maize to boiling water and stir well. When the mixture forms a mass, add butter if desired. Stir well, then cover for 2 to 4 minutes. Continue to stir occasionally for 10 minutes and place in a bowl. Serve while still hot, each person slicing off his portion. An interesting variation: divide the Ugali into two bowls; add 4 tablespoons butter to one and serve the other plain. Stir and serve both as directed.

Jane Ogwayo
Nairobi, Kenya

Ugali is a cornmeal staple in Kenya.

ISRAEL

3rd Week of December
HANUKKAH

Hanukkah — the Festival of Lights — while perhaps not as holy for Israeli believers as Rosh Hashanah (Day of Remembrance) or Yom Kippur (Day of Atonement), is important because it symbolizes the heroic struggle of the few over the mighty. In 165 B.C., Maccabean zealots defeated stronger Syrian forces and recaptured the temple in Jerusalem. As a rededication, with only a day's supply of oil on hand, the victors lit the temple's menorah (candelabrum) — their one vial miraculously lasting for eight days.

Over time, Hanukkah evolved from a minor event of the winter solstice into a major family festival. While the candles burn, no work is allowed; special songs and rejoicing are encouraged. From the Maccabean town of Modi'in, torches representing religious freedom are carried by runners to all parts of the country.

When Hanukkah begins, the Jewish family gathers to light the first candle on a nine-branched menorah. From this first Shamesh candle an additional one or more, increasing to eight, will be lit on each of eight nights. Children receive "Hanukkah gelt," money or a longed-for gift. The evening meal might include the eastern Mediterranean holiday breads Challah and Babka — or, to remind them of the "miracle of the oil," fried foods like doughnuts or latkes, perhaps the ultimate Jewish comfort food. After enjoying a children's festival, they might serve Hanukkah sugar cookies shaped like menorahs, airy and crunchy Kichel, or Rugalach, cream-cheese pastries with cinnamon, nut, and raisin filling.

Hanukkah also calls for the traditional and riotous game of chance using a spinning top called a dreidel, the four sides of which bear the Hebrew letters N, G, H, and S — the acronym for "a miracle happened here."

LATKES
(Potato Pancakes)

5 large or 8 medium potatoes
1 or 2 large onions (optional)
3 eggs
5 tablespoons flour
Salt and white pepper to taste

Peel and grate potatoes and onions, press out excess moisture, and add other ingredients, mixing well. Flatten heaping tablespoons of the mixture into 2- or 3-inch rounds and fry on each side in 1 inch of hot vegetable oil until crisp and golden. Drain on paper towels and serve with applesauce, sour cream, or yogurt.

Rachel Peleg
Raanana, Israel

Easy Israeli Chicken with honey pleases Mina Shachaf's visitors.

Visitors to the town of Shefar'am discover an Arab community with three separate cultural identities. Whether Christian, Muslim, or Druse, daily life revolves around the family unit and hospitality to visitors is customary. Holidays also differ widely: in early December Christian Arabs observe Advent in preparation for Christmas, while the important Muslim feasts take place in the spring months.

The welcome reception for a Friendship Force group is usually a meal served at the House of Hope, the first international peace center initiated by Arabs in the Middle East.

Heyam Jabbour, center, of Shefar'am in Upper Galilee, prepares dinner with help from relatives.

EASY ISRAELI CHICKEN

1 1/2 tablespoons chicken bouillon granules
6 chicken leg quarters or chicken breasts
2 or 3 tablespoons honey
6 tablespoons soy sauce

Mix bouillon granules with hot water as directed. Add all ingredients in a kettle with enough water to cover the chicken. Simmer for 2 hours or more until chicken pieces are tender, occasionally turning them within the broth so all will cook evenly. If chicken breasts are used, less cooking time may be needed.

Mina Shachaf
Ashkelon, Israel

TABOULI

1 1/2 cups bulgar (cracked wheat)
3 green onions or scallions, finely chopped
1/3 to 1/2 cup mint, finely chopped
Olive oil
Lemon juice

Wash the bulgar, squeeze out water, and let stand for 1/2 hour until soft, adding more water if needed. Squeeze again. Lightly cover chopped onions and mint with olive oil and let stand for 1/2 hour. Mix ingredients together and sprinkle with lemon juice. Serve on Romaine lettuce as a salad, wrap in lettuce leaves as a finger food, or serve as a pita bread filler with condiments of choice.

Lina Shehadeh
Shefar'am, Upper Galilee, Israel

TAHINI SQUASH AND HUMMUS
(Squash and Chickpea Dips)

Tahini Squash and Hummus are Middle Eastern dishes served as a dip from a common or individual bowls. One tears off a bit of bread — usually warmed pieces of pita bread — or uses chips, and scoops a generous mouthful as with any dip. These dishes can also be eaten with a spoon.

TAHINI SQUASH

2 or 3 large butternut or acorn squash
1 rounded tablespoon tahini (sesame butter) for each
*   cup of squash meat*
1 tablespoon pure olive oil
1 clove garlic
1 tablespoon fresh lemon juice

Wash, halve, and remove seeds from the squash. Boil, then simmer in water, covered, until the squash meat can be scooped with a spoon. (Cool in the pan to lukewarm to make scooping easier.) In a large bowl, stir until well mashed. Add tahini, stir, and watch the magic as the squash becomes a fluffy creamy texture and the color lightens. Add remaining 3 ingredients and blend until smooth and well mixed. Vary seasonings to taste and serve chilled or hot. Keeps several days in the refrigerator and also freezes well.

HUMMUS

Instead of squash, use 2 one-pound cans of chickpeas or garbanzos. Discard liquid from one can; put the remainder of both into a blender and gradually blend to a creamy consistency. Add 2 to 3 tablespoons tahini, 1 tablespoon each olive oil and lemon juice and 1 clove garlic. Blend until smooth and adjust seasonings to taste. Serve chilled and garnish if desired.

Note: Sesame butter (tahini) can be made by lightly toasting several ounces of sesame seeds on a cookie pan and blending them into a paste, adding enough olive oil to smooth to a peanut-butter consistency.

Heyam Jabbour
Shefar'am, Upper Galilee, Israel

Tabouli is a favorite throughout the Mediterranean area.

COSTA RICA

Christmas in Costa Rica begins a few days before December 25 with the construction of the most important seasonal decorations, the Navidad Portal. Following its own tradition, each family sets up the scene where Jesus was born on the first Christmas. There might be colored lights and mountains made from thick colored paper; moss or cotton snow might cover the ground; and a ceramic mule or bull might keep the lambs company. Each nativity scene has a Virgin Mary, St. Joseph, and an angel hung on high, while three wise men wait to one side.

On the 24th, men are invited to join the women-folk in the tamalada — making the traditional tamales for the Noche Buena family dinner. Some will prepare plantain leaves to hold the tamales, while others blend the dough or the filling. A warm drink called Aguadulce will be made from boiling sugarcane, lime juice, and sugar. The Christmas Bread will be unwrapped and dusted with powdered sugar.

Most Costa Ricans attend church on Christmas Eve. Just before leaving for the midnight Misa del Gallo ("roosters mass"), a family prayer will be said as the figure of Baby Jesus is added to the manger.

Dinner before or after Mass will include tamales; other meats such as Arroz Con Pollo (chicken and rice pilaf), stuffed loin, or turkey; many vegetables and salads, and the fragrant Christmas Bread and fruitcake. Tables are covered in red or green cloths and red-splashed poinsettias.

After lunch on Christmas Day, Costa Ricans visit with friends, exchange gifts, and admire what San Nicolas left for the children. And, even in a country where families gather every weekend, they remember with fondness the special magic of Noche Buena.

TAMALES DE CERDO
(Pork Tamales with Vegetables)

1 1/2 pounds boneless pork shoulder

1 small chicken

Salt, pepper, garlic and salsa lizano (steak sauce)

2 pounds potatoes, cooked and mashed

*4 cups masa rica (maseca, instant corn flour), mixed
    with 2 1/4 cups water*

4 tablespoons pork fat or margarine, melted

1 cup yellow or white rice

Ochiote to taste (similar to paprika)

*4 pounds plantain leaves, cleaned and softened in
    boiling water, or 24 squares aluminum foil about
    8″ x 8″*

2 green peppers, cut in long strips

8 ounces dried chickpeas, lightly cooked

1 cup canned or frozen peas

2 small carrots, sliced lengthwise

Raisins and olives (optional)

Boil pork and chicken in water seasoned as desired with salt, pepper, garlic, and salsa lizano; cut into small pieces. Mash potatoes with enough warm meat broth to make a fairly soft dough when added to the maseca and melted margarine. Blend this mixture by hand until the dough is rather soft but not dry.

Prepare rice according to directions and add ochiote. Do not overcook. In the center of two plantain leaves (or foil) place 2 tablespoons of raw masa dough, 1 tablespoon rice, 1 pepper strip, 4 chickpeas, 1 tablespoon chicken and pork, 1 teaspoon peas, 1 carrot strip and, if desired, 1 olive and 4 raisins.

When tamales are wrapped into squares, stack

one on top of a second one. Tie the pair with string, both across and from top to bottom. Place in a large pot of boiling water and simmer for 1 hour. Drain and serve warm with a cup of black coffee. Makes 24.

Tamales may be frozen or refrigerated. Reheat in boiling water or in a microwave oven if foil has not been used.

Alice Alpizar, Margarita Ugalde,
and Lenny Vilafuerte Moreno
Alajuela, Costa Rica

ROMPOPE
(Costa Rican Eggnog)

1 quart milk
2 eggs, beaten
Cinnamon to taste
Sugar to taste
Pinch of salt
2 tablespoons cornstarch in 1/2 cup water
Rum or guaro

Mix the first 5 ingredients and bring to a boil, stirring constantly. Then add cornstarch mixed with water. Continue to stir until the mixture thickens. Cool and add desired amount of rum or guaro. Serve cold. Makes 10 cups.

Flora Jara
Alajuela, Costa Rica

Poinsettias surround a Costa Rican favorite for Christmas Eve, Torta de Navidad, or Christmas Bread.

TORTA DE NAVIDAD
(Christmas Bread)

1/2 pound (1 cup) butter or margarine
3/4 cup sugar
1/8 teaspoon salt or less
1 cup hot milk
1 cup flour
3 tablespoons dry yeast in 1/4 cup warm water
3 eggs, beaten
Grated peel of 1 lemon
1/2 cup candied pineapple and cherries
1/2 cup raisins
2 teaspoons cinnamon
1 teaspoon vanilla
4 cups flour or more
Powdered sugar

Blend butter, sugar, and salt into the hot milk. Add 1 cup flour and the dissolved yeast. Place in an oiled pan, cover with a cloth and allow to rise in a warm place. Then add eggs, grated lemon, fruit, cinnamon, and vanilla. Add remaining flour a little at a time until the dough is not sticky. Shape into loaves, place in greased loaf pans, cover, and allow to rise until double in size. Bake in a preheated 350° F oven for 1/2 hour or until done. While still warm, dust with powdered sugar.

Note: Costa Rican families begin making Christmas Bread in early December. Wrapped in foil, they are opened every other day and a spoonful of rum is poured on.

Carlos Herra
Alajuela, Costa Rica

POLAND

4th Week of December
WIGILIA DINNER

In Poland Christmas begins with a special Christmas Eve dinner called Wigilia. Old traditions call for the family to gather in the dining area by the Christmas tree, gaily decorated with old straw ornaments. A white tablecloth symbolizing Mary covers a handful of hay, to remind everyone of Jesus' birth in a stable. The head of the family passes around a large thin wafer for each to break off a portion; in a beautiful tradition, when the wafer is shared, it has the power of mutual forgiveness and reconciliation. An empty chair at the table is reserved for Christ or an unexpected guest. In many homes, garlands hung from the four corners of the room signify the four corners of the earth.

Even the Wigilia menu is traditional. It usually contains 13 servings to represent Christ and the apostles. Fish dishes constitute the main entrées and might include carp, fried or in aspic; salted herrings; and perhaps pike simmered in vegetable broth topped with chopped eggs, butter, and parsley. The usual soup course is Barszcz Wigilijny and Uszka — borscht made from beets and poured over mushroom ravioli. This might be followed by Pierogi, dumplings stuffed with cabbage.

Most desserts are based on poppy seeds, dried fruits, and nuts, such as Waffles with Poppy Seeds or a variety called Kutia. Christmas gingerbread and spicy cakes like Piernik are popular, and oranges are a special treat for the children. The special Wigilia drink is a chilled fruit compote served in a bowl.

The Wigilia dinner ends for the Polish family when they gather around the tree to open presents.

BARSZCZ WIGILIJNY AND USZKA
(Beetroot Soup and Mushroom Ravioli)

1:

3 1/2 pounds beetroots

2 quarts water

1 tablespoon salt

2 or 3 cloves garlic

2:

3 to 4 ounces dried wild mushrooms

3 to 4 cups water

3:

3 to 4 pounds fresh beetroots

2 carrots

1 onion

1 each: celery root and leek

1 parsley root or white parsnip root

2 to 3 cups water

Salt and pepper

4:

3 tablespoons onions, peeled and cut into small cubes

1 teaspoon butter or olive oil

Salt and pepper

1 tablespoon fine bread crumbs

5:

1 1/4 cups flour

1 egg

1/2 cup water

STEP 1: Peel beets, cut into pieces, and place in a pottery jar. Add water, salt, and garlic. Cover with cheesecloth to allow air to enter and set aside in a cool room for 7 to 10 days. Stir, discard beets, and reserve the liquid.

STEP 2: Soak mushrooms in water overnight; next day cook until tender. Remove mushrooms and set aside. Reserve the liquid.

STEP 3: Clean and cut the fresh beets. Combine with vegetables in enough water to cover. Boil until vegetables are tender and a clear red broth results. Remove the vegetables and chop, setting them aside to serve as a side dish, if desired. Mix the vegetable liquid with mushroom juice (step 2) and add fermented juice (step 1) a little at a time until the desired sourness is reached. Put liquids through a sieve; add salt and pepper to taste. Keep warm but do not boil. If the color fades, add the juice of 1 lemon.

STEP 4: Sauté onions in butter until golden. Grind onions with mushrooms (step 2) in a food processor. Add salt and pepper to taste. Add fine bread crumbs and mix well to make a fine paste.

STEP 5: Mix and knead a soft dough from flour, egg and water, as for dumplings. Roll until thin and cut into 1 1/2-inch squares. Place mushroom paste on each square, fold diagonally, and pinch edges together to form a triangle. Bend two of the angles of the triangle and stick one over the other in the center. Cook several at a time in a large pot of salted water, stirring. When they come to the surface, remove with a slotted spoon and repeat the process. To serve, place 5 or 6 Uszkas in a deep plate or soup bowl. Pour the hot soup, or borscht, over them.

Justyna Bukowska
Warsaw, Poland

WIGILIJNY KOMPOT
(Wigilia Fruit Compote)

8 to 10 ounces dried pitted prunes
8 to 10 ounces dried figs
2 tablespoons sugar, divided
1 cinnamon stick
Juice of 1 lemon and strips of rind

Rinse prunes in lukewarm water, drain, and add enough cold water to cover. Soak for 12 hours overnight. In a separate bowl, do the same with figs. Next day, add half the sugar and the cinnamon stick to the prunes and bring to a boil in the soak water for 1 minute. To the figs, add the remaining sugar, lemon juice, and 2 or 3 narrow strips of rind. Bring to a boil and cook for 5 minutes. To serve, remove the cinnamon stick and lemon rind and combine the fruit. Place in glass bowls or crystal glasses and serve at room temperature after the Christmas Eve Wigilia dinner.

Elizabeth G. Krawczynska
Warsaw, Poland, and Atlanta, Georgia

Elizabeth Krawczynska ladles into bowls her Christmas Eve compote of figs and prunes.

UKRAINE

5th Week of December
ORTHODOX CHRISTMAS

During the forty days preceding Orthodox Christmas in the Ukraine, Christians prepare themselves for this most holy of days by abstaining from meat, milk, and eggs.

The Ukraine attained independence in 1991 after almost 80 years as one of the 15 republics in the Soviet Union. In the years since, church attendance has flourished, with 40 churches in Kiev and at least one in each village. The morning service on Orthodox Christmas — January 7 on the western calendar — is crowded and joyous. The solemn ritual lasts for three hours, during which "Christmas Water" is blessed for use all year by the sick. As choirs sing exultantly about the birth of Jesus, a most happy day begins for Ukrainian families.

Back at home, children find their gifts under the decorated tree. Then the family gathers for Christmas dinner; another smaller tree adorned with glass toys and other ornaments is centered on the white tablecloth. Another linen cloth is laid under each plate, and a red candle is lit to bring gladness to the heart. Since meat has been absent from the diet for so many weeks, the main course might be a veal roast or Kiev Kruchiniki, served with rice and vegetable salads which include potatoes.

After dinner, an impromptu serenade of Christmas songs at the homes of neighbors and friends completes the festive day.

Although apple pie might follow dinner on Christmas day, the most traditional dessert is served to each member of the family on Christmas Eve. A tasty dish called Kutia is popular throughout eastern Europe. It is made by soaking wheat grain in water for several hours; cooking it for two more hours; and then mixing it with honey, poppy seeds, raisins, crushed nuts, and a cold compote made from dried fruits.

KIEV KRUCHENIKI

2 pounds veal or fine beef
Salt and pepper as needed
2 ounces or more mushrooms
1/2 cup chopped onion
3 hard-boiled eggs, chopped
1 can (14 ounces) mushroom, beef, or chicken broth
4 tablespoons flour
4 tablespoons (1/4 cup) butter
8 ounces sour cream

Ask the butcher to cut the meat into 6 large slices, thin enough to roll; tenderize and add salt and pepper. Spread the top of each piece of meat with Mushroom Stuffing, roll, and bind with cotton thread. Place in a well-greased baking dish, add half the broth, cover, and bake for 1 hour in a preheated 350° F oven. To serve, remove meat rolls to a warm

Stuffed and rolled beef and mushroom sauce wait to be cooked in the Romanchenko kitchen.

platter (reserve pan juices) and cover with Mushroom Sauce. If desired, return to the warm oven for a few minutes. Serves 6.

MUSHROOM STUFFING

Wash mushrooms and cut into small pieces. Fry onion until golden, mix with mushrooms; add salt, pepper, and chopped eggs. (Dried mushrooms may be used.)

MUSHROOM SAUCE

Blend flour into melted butter; over low heat, add remaining broth, liquid from the pan, and additional water if needed. When thickened enough, blend in sour cream and any mushrooms that remain.

Helen Romanchenko
Kiev, Ukraine

Tonya Romanchenko, left, and her daughter-in-law, Helen Romanchenko, happily present one of their Ukrainian dishes for inspection.

WINTER VEGETABLE SALAD

1 pound potatoes, boiled
5 to 6 ounces green peas, fresh or frozen, slightly cooked

1/4 medium sour cabbage, chopped and marinated in vinegar
1/2 cup onions, chopped
3 medium carrots, slightly cooked
1 teaspoon salt and pepper to taste
6 to 8 ounces sour cream, divided
2 tablespoons hot mustard
Parsley

Cut boiled potatoes; add green peas, sour cabbage (marinated in vinegar), onions, carrots, and salt and pepper. Add 6 ounces sour cream blended with mustard. Spread 2 ounces sour cream on top and decorate with parsley. Or place a rose rolled from apple peels in the center and surround it with notched carrot slices, a sprinkle of peas, and tomato slices. Serves 4 to 6.

Tonya Romanchenko
Kiev, Ukraine

MIXED CREAM WITH SUGAR

8 ounces (1 cup) sour cream
1/4 cup sugar, or as desired
8 ounces (1 cup) fresh cream, whipped
Rum or other liquor
Toppings to decorate

Mix sour cream and sugar. Fold into the whipped cream. Pour rum or other liquor into individual serving glasses; add the mixed cream and decorate with chocolate shavings, pecans, raisins, or a slice of lemon. Caramel or another sauce may also be used. Serve with cold orange juice or lemonade.

Tonya Romanchenko

VISITS TO OTHER INTERNATIONAL KITCHENS

This worldwide culinary tour has been one of festivals, everyday meals and special family times. The Friendship Force hopes its members — and fellow cooks around the world — will use this calendar to share a weekly meal and a holiday with their international friends as often as they can through the year.

To further tease appetites with food from other lands, the following dishes are presented to give readers a taste from additional countries and U.S. regions. These recipes come from Friendship Force members in Belarus, Louisiana, Denmark, Kentucky, Northern Ireland, South Korea, and Vietnam — and each has come to define the cuisine of that region.

DRANIKI
(Potato Pancakes)

Since potatoes are a basic crop in Belarus, formerly part of the U.S.S.R., it is not surprising that they are widely used in Belarusian cooking. One very popular cookbook in Belarus includes 500 potato dishes. Draniki is an everyday main dish as well as one fit for a festive table when served with meat or fish. Galina Petkevich of Minsk describes Draniki as popular, typical of her country, and "most democratic since it does not contain any expensive ingredients."

8 to 10 medium-size potatoes
3 tablespoons flour
Salt to taste
1 or 2 eggs or one of the following:
  1/3 cup sour milk
  2 to 3 tablespoons mayonnaise

Process potatoes with a fine shredder, add flour and salt, and one of the three variants (egg, sour milk, or mayonnaise). The mixture must be thick enough to allow the pancakes to hold their shape.

Drop the mixture in large spoonfuls onto a heated griddle, greased with vegetable oil, and fry. To serve, pour melted butter over the pancakes and provide sour cream at the table.

For a more festive meal, brown 1/2 pound of ground pork together with 2 chopped onions. Set aside and make the Draniki. When pancakes are ready, put a layer of browned pork and onions between each pair of pancakes and keep them warm in the oven before serving. With this variant, use no melted butter or sauce.

Galina Petkevich,
Minsk, Belarus

Graciela Wilson of Chile talks with Inger Rice, right, about her recipe for Danish Frikadeller.

FRIKADELLER
(Danish Meatballs)

Inger Rice of Virginia, a longtime member of the Friendship Force Board of Directors, considers Frikadeller to be the national dish of her native country, Denmark.

1/2 pound each: ground beef, ground veal, and ground pork
1 large onion, chopped
1/2 teaspoon each: salt and pepper
1/4 cup flour
1/4 cup Italian bread crumbs
2 cups milk
2 eggs, beaten
Butter for frying

Put the combined meats through a meat grinder, then repeat twice more with the onions. Add salt, pepper, flour, bread crumbs, and milk to the mixture and blend well with the electric mixer. Continue mixing for 3 to 4 minutes while adding eggs. Set aside in a cool place for 30 minutes.

Melt butter in a frying pan. First coating a spoon in butter, scoop spoonfuls of the meat mixture and place in the frying pan. Flatten each oblong meatball slightly with the spoon. Fry on medium to high heat until brown on each side, about 8 minutes per side. Makes 12 meatballs.

Inger Rice
Richmond, Virginia

SAUSAGE AND SHRIMP JAMBALAYA

Geraldine Beaird describes Cajun food as a mixture of French, Caribbean, African, and American —

with ingredients found in any garden or bayou. Cajun culture is hospitable and flexible; adding a cup of water or rice allows unexpected visitors to share in this favorite staple for a family gathering.

2 pounds smoked or cooked sausage, cut into bite-size pieces
3 large onions, chopped
1 bell pepper, chopped (optional)
3 stalks celery, chopped
3 cloves garlic, chopped
1 bunch green onions, chopped
1/4 cup chopped parsley
3 cups water
1 can (15 ounces) tomatoes, cut and mashed
1 teaspoon salt, or to taste
Ground red pepper to taste
2 cups raw rice
1 pound shrimp, peeled

In a large iron pot, brown sausage and sauté onions until clear. Add bell pepper, celery, garlic, green onions, and parsley and sauté together over low heat for 10 minutes or until limp. Add water, tomatoes, salt, and red pepper and bring to a boil. Add rice and shrimp. Stir and turn heat to low. Cover and simmer for 30 to 40 minutes. If the mixture sticks, add a bit more water. Serves 10 to 12.

Geraldine Beaird
Baton Rouge, Louisiana

KENTUCKY MINT JULEPS

Mary Alice Blanton shares this Louisville tradition with Kentucky Derby race week visitors or with Friendship Force Ambassador guests who visit at other times and want to experience the renowned libation.

1 cup water
2 cups sugar
1/2 cup packed mint leaves
2 cups Kentucky Bourbon
Crushed ice
Mint sprigs

To make simple syrup: boil water and sugar for 5 minutes. When cool, add mint leaves and allow to steep overnight or for 12 hours, stirring occasionally. Strain the syrup through a fine sieve and discard the mint.

To make juleps: combine bourbon and 1 cup of the minted simple syrup. Chill overnight or until needed; the mixture should be very cold. To serve, place a short straw in each sterling silver julep cup or tumbler and arrange mint sprigs around the straw, so that the nose draws bouquet from the mint leaves. Fill cups or tumblers with crushed ice and add the chilled, minted bourbon.

Mary Alice Blanton
Louisville, Kentucky

IRISH STEW

Kathleen Irwin, secretary of The Friendship Force of the Causeway Coast in Northern Ireland, believes this recipe well represents the cuisine of her country. For many Irish immigrants to America in the mid-19th century, it was a family staple.

1 pound scrag-end neck of mutton or lamb
2 pounds potatoes
1 pound onions
Water for boiling
Salt and pepper to taste

Wipe the meat and cut into neat pieces. Wash and peel potatoes and cut into slices or cubes. Peel and slice onions. Place all three into a stewpan in layers, add salt and pepper, and water to barely cover and slowly bring to a boil. Simmer for 1 1/2 to 2 hours, stirring occasionally. Serve on a hot platter with potatoes arranged around the meat. Cover with gravy made from the meat juices.

Kathleen Irvin
County Antrim, Northern Ireland

KOREAN KIMCHEE

Every Friendship Force visitor to Korea returns home exclaiming about Kimchee, the traditional spicy pickled vegetables served at every meal. Members in Washington State were first to visit Korea in 1978 and 1979. Returning with memories of delicious food, Eleanor Van Tilburg and Marijane Brown developed their own Korean dishes with help from Korean friends. In the years since, they have presented Korean meals on many occasions.

1 head Chinese cabbage
2 tablespoons plus 1 teaspoon salt
5-inch piece daikon radish or 1 bunch icicle radish
6 green onions, including tops
4 cloves garlic
2 tablespoons crushed Korean chili peppers
1 tablespoon freshly grated gingerroot
Optional: coarsely grated carrot, sliced turnips, celery, etc.
1 cup water

Slice Chinese cabbage into 2-inch lengths. In a large glass or stainless steel bowl, sprinkle 2 tablespoons salt over cabbage and mix by hand. Let stand overnight, then drain and wash cabbage well with cold water. Drain again.

Grate radish, slice green onions into 2-inch lengths, and crush garlic. With your hands, mix cabbage and other ingredients, including 1 teaspoon salt. (To avoid eye injury, wash hands after handling chili pepper.)

Place the mixture in a large glass or metal bowl (not aluminum) or pack into pint or quart jars. Cover loosely and let stand at room temperature for about 5 days. (Kimchee made in warm summer months takes only 2 to 3 days to ferment.) Refrigerate. Kimchee will keep for several weeks in the refrigerator. It is served as a relish at every meal.

Eleanor Van Tilburg, Ridgefield, Washington
Marijane Brown, Vancouver, Washington

COM CHIEN
(Vietnamese Fried Rice)

Members of the Vietnam Union of Friendship Organizations helped to organize the first visit of Hanoi Vietnamese to Big Canoe, Georgia, in June of 1995. This visit was preceded by Friendship Force Ambassadors traveling to Vietnam over Thanksgiving, 1993, and in the spring of 1994. They found that rice and rice noodles are staples of the Vietnamese diet. Com Chien includes everything needed for a nutritious meal.

4 cups rice
4 tablespoons vegetable oil
2 eggs, beaten well
1/2 medium onion, chopped
1 carrot, chopped
2/3 cup fresh or frozen green peas
1 cup cooked ham, diced
Pepper to taste
1 teaspoon sugar
2 teaspoons fish sauce
1 teaspoon soy sauce

Cook the rice and set aside to cool. In a saucepan over medium heat, add 1 tablespoon of oil. When hot, add beaten eggs and quickly scramble them with a fork. Remove to a plate and set aside. Add the remaining oil to the skillet and sauté the onions for 2 minutes, stirring often. Add carrots and peas, cover, and cook the vegetables for 5 minutes. Add ham pieces, pepper, sugar, and the two sauces and stir well. Finally, add the cooled rice and break apart any clumps. After mixing thoroughly, cook for 5 to 10 minutes to completely heat the mixture. Just before serving, add scrambled egg pieces and again mix well. Serve hot. For 4 persons.

Tran Minh Quoc,
Vietnam

Kathleen Irwin of Northern Ireland finds a good spot by the rocky north shore to prepare Irish Stew.

METRICS

FLUID MEASUREMENTS

American Measure	Fluid Ounces	Approximate Metric (Milliliters)
1 teaspoon	1/6 ounce	1 teaspoon (5 ml)
2 teaspoons	1/3 ounce	1 dessert teaspoon (10 ml)
1 Tablespoon	1/2 ounce	1 Tablespoon (15 ml)
2 Tablespoons	1 ounce	2 Tablespoons (30 ml)
1/4 cup: 4 Tablespoons	2 ounces	4 Tablespoons (59 ml)
1/3 cup: 5.25 Tablespoons	2 2/3 oz	5 Tablespoons (79 ml)
1/2 cup: 8 Tablespoons	4 ounces	8 Tablespoons (118 ml; 1.2 dl)
1 cup	8 ounces	1/4 liter
2 cups: 1 pint	16 ounces	1/2 liter (473 ml or scant 5 dl)
4 cups: 1 quart	32 ounces	scant 1 liter

SOLID MEASUREMENTS

American (Ounces and Pounds)	Approximate Metric (Grams)
1/3 ounce	10 grams/1 dkg
1 ounce	28 grams
2 ounce	56 grams
3 1/2 ounces; 7 Tablespoons	100 grams
4 ounces; 1/4 pound	114 grams
8 ounces; 1/2 pound	226 grams
9 ounces	255 grams/1/4 kilogram
12 ounces; 3/4 pound	340 grams
16 ounces; 1 pound	450 grams
2 1/4 pounds	1000 grams/1 kilo

OVEN TEMPERATURE AND APPROXIMATE EQUIVALENTS

Fahrenheit:	Celsius:	Gas mark:	Description:
275	140	1	Very slow
300	150	2	
325	170	3	Slow
350	180	4	Moderate
375	190	5	
400	205	6	Moderately hot
425	220	7	Fairly hot
450	230	8	Hot
475	245	9	Very hot
500	260	10	Extremely hot

MEASUREMENTS IN INCHES AND CENTIMETERS

Inches	Centimeters	Inches	Centimeters
3/8 inch	1 cm	1 inch	2 1/2 cm
1/2 inch	1 1/2 cm	9 inches	23 cm
3/4 inch	2 cm	10 inches	25 1/2 cm

MEASUREMENTS AND SUBSTITUTIONS

2 egg yolks or whites	1 egg
1 cup flour	4 1/2 ounces or 125 grams
1 cup granulated sugar	6 ounces or 170 grams
1 cup confectioners' sugar	4 1/2 ounces or 125 grams
1 cup loose brown sugar	6 ounces or 170 grams
1 cup sour milk	1 cup milk with 1T vinegar
1 tablespoon cornstarch	2 tablespoons flour (for thickening)
1 teaspoon baking powder	1/4 teaspoon soda + 1/2 tsp cream of tartar
1 cup milk	1/2 cup evaporated + 1/2 cup water
1 cup milk	4 tablespoons powdered milk + 1 cup water
1/2 pound cheese	2 cups grated cheese
1/2 pint whipping cream	2 cups whipped cream
1 medium lemon	3 tablespoons juice
1 packet dry yeast	1 tablespoon; 1/4 ounce; 1 cake
a pinch	less than 1/8 teaspoon

Note: When measuring one cup of flour or sugar, it is difficult to get the same reading in ounces each time it is measured. The above amounts represent the average reading for flour and sugar. Individual cooks should adjust the amounts of ingredients if and whenever necessary.

EQUIVALENTS AND DESCRIPTIONS

All-purpose flour	Plain wheat flour
Self-rising flour	Flour with 1/2 teaspoon salt and 1 teaspoon baking powder added per cup
Confectioners' sugar	Powdered sugar or icing sugar
Cornstarch	Cornflour
Cream	Single: light cream Double: heavy or whipping cream Half and half: milk with 12% fat
Castor sugar	Fine granulated sugar
Shortening	White fat, lard or margarine
Vanilla essence	Vanilla flavoring; also pod or bean

ACKNOWLEDGMENTS

The Friendship Force thanks the following for their assistance.

THE RECIPE COMMITTEE:

Co-Chairpersons: Beverlie J. Reilman, Atlanta, Georgia
Jeanne Comer - Dayton, Ohio
Mary Alice Blanton - Louisville, Kentucky
Trudy Martin - Langley, Washington

Toko Yomura, Tokyo, Japan
Virginia Smith - Birmingham, Alabama
Alice Josephson - Cocoa Beach, Florida
Martha and Mary Pace - Lithonia, Georgia

THE CLUBS WHOSE MEMBERS TESTED RECIPES:

The Friendship Force of Atlanta South, Georgia
The Friendship Force of Birmingham, Alabama
The Friendship Force of Dayton, Ohio
The Friendship Force of Pau, France
The Friendship Force of Tokyo, Japan

The Friendship Force of Big Canoe, Georgia
The Friendship Force of Cardiff, Wales
The Friendship Force of Greater Louisville, Kentucky
The Friendship Force of Quad-Cities, Iowa and Illinois
The Friendship Force of Whidbey Island, Washington

SECRETARIAL ASSISTANCE, PROOFING, TESTING AND RECIPES:

Melenie Dickinson
Betty Donato
Rubye Erickson
Wilma Gray
Miriam Henriksen
Mary Kitchens
and especially: Alice Josephson, Mary Pace and Martha Pace

Ruth McLeod
Queenie Ross
Patricia Stephenson
Lucille Wilson
Bill Lamkin

PHOTO CREDITS:

Paolo Bellardo, Piacenza, Italy (March cover and page 35)
Art Bryant, Lincoln, Nebraska (August cover).
Jim Conway, Atlanta, Georgia (photo of the Carters).
Stewart Crawford, Wanganui, New Zealand (May cover and pages 58 and 60). Robert Hewitt, Colorado Springs, Colorado (page 17).
Bill Hopkins, Des Moines, Iowa (page 101).
Bob Kagey, Santa Barbara, California (page 64).
Bill Lamkin, Atlanta, Georgia (page 151).
The Picture Gallery, Cleveland, England (November cover).
Beverlie Reilman, Atlanta, Georgia.
Larry Thomas Photography, Atlanta, Georgia (January, February, June, July, September, October and December covers and pages 7 and 81).
Malulee Pinsuvana, Bangkok, Thailand (April cover and pages 48 and 50).
The Atlanta Speech School and Bobby Libby, Jacksonville, Florida (page 136).
National Turkey Federation
and those members who photographed themselves and their food.

ALSO: "Come to Our Salmon Feast" by Martha Ferguson McKeown, Binfords and Mort Publishers, Portland, Oregon, 1959.

Konafa (Filo Dough Dessert)	Egypt	47
Lekvar (Apricot Jam)	Hungary	104
Lemon Custard Pie	Colombia	6
Mexican Sheet Cake	U.S.A.	41
Mixed Cream with Sugar	Ukraine	158
Mote de Huesillos (Peaches)	Chile	114
Nanimo Bars	Canada	84
Olde English Sherry Trifle	England	141
Pavlova #1	New Zealand	59
Pavlova #2	New Zealand	60
Peanutty Rainbow Cookies	U.S.A.	112
Pepernoten (Ginger Nuts)	Netherlands	147
Praline Pecan Pie	U.S.A.	143
Revani (Syrup Cake)	Turkey	129
Rhubarb Strawberry Cobbler	Canada	84
Scandinavian Puff	Sweden	79
Sopa Pillas (Pastry)	Peru	95
South African Silk (Mousse)	South Africa	53
Speculaas (Christmas Cookies)	Netherlands	145
Tarte Tatin (Apple Tart)	France	91
Teisennau Afal (Apple Cakes)	Wales	32
Wigilijny (Fruit Compote)	Poland	156
Wine Cream	Germany	125

DRINKS

Bisschopswijn	Netherlands	147
Caipirinha	Brazil	81
Irish Coffee	Ireland	37
Kentucky Mint Juleps	U.S.A.	160
Peach Champagne Soup	U.S.A.	134
Rompope (Eggnog)	Costa Rica	154
Spiced Wassail	U.S.A.	20
St. Patrick's Day Cider Cup	Ireland	36

EGGS, CHEESE AND CURDS

Ann's Macaroni and Cheese	U.S.A.	70
Camarao com Catupiry with Cream Cheese	Brazil	81
Chawan Mushi (Egg Custard with Chicken and Shrimp)	Japan	4
Cheese Fondue	U.S.A.	17
Cheese Puffs with Olives	U.S.A.	65
Gnocchi di Patate al Formaggio (Potato Dumplings and Cheese)	Italy	34
Paskha (Molded Curd Dish)	Russia	44
Soleier (Eggs in Salt Water)	Germany	125

FISH AND SEAFOOD

Bantry Bay Fish Soup	Ireland	37
Barbecued Salmon in Lemon and White Wine	U.S.A.	106
Camarao com Catupiry (Shrimp with Cream Cheese)	Chile	81
Chawan Mushi (Egg Custard with Chicken and Shrimp)	Japan	4
Fish Casserole	Kenya	148
Kazunoko (Herring Roe)	Japan	3
Marinated Salmon Smorbrod	Norway	62
Mee Grob (Crispy Noodles)	Thailand	50
Midye Dolmasi (Stuffed Mussels)	Turkey	130
Moules Mariniere (Mussels)	Belgium	93
Naam Prig Pla Yaang (Grilled Fish Dip)	Thailand	48
Pickled Herring	Sweden	78
Prawn Cocktail	Australia	15
Sate (Marinated Shrimp)	Indonesia	25
Sausage and Shrimp Jambalaya	U.S.A.	160
Sewin with Cucumber Sauce	Wales	33
Smoked Salmon Casserole	Ireland	36
Spargelsuppe mit Krabben (Asparagus Soup with Shrimp)	Germany	124
Tarbot met Champagnesaus (Turbot in Champagne Sauce)	Belgium	92
Tatsukuri (Dried Sardines)	Japan	3

Tom Yum Goong (Sour Shrimp Soup)	Thailand	49
Ukoy (Shrimp Fritters)	Philippines	76
Yusheng (Raw Fish Salad)	Singapore	22
Zoni (Fish Soup)	Japan	3

GRAINS AND POTATOES

Arroz con Cola a la Colombiana (White Rice with Cola)	Colombia	6
Com Chien (Fried Rice)	Vietnam	162
Draniki (Potato Pancakes)	Belarus	159
Gnocchi di Patate al Formaggio (Potato Dumplings and Cheese)	Italy	34
Gratin Dauphinois (Potatoes au Gratin)	France	91
Khichdi (Vegetable Biryani)	India	8
Khinkali (Meat Dumplings)	Georgia	127
Klimbisupp (Meat Soup with Dumplings)	Estonia	28
Knedlik (Dumplings)	Czech Rep.	118
Kpekpele (Steamed Cornmeal)	Ghana	98
Latkes (Potato Pancakes)	Israel	150
Mee Grob (Crispy Noodles)	Thailand	50
Nasi Goreng (Fried Rice)	Indonesia	26
Papa a la Huancaina (Potatoes with Cream Sauce)	Peru	95
Papas Chorreadas (Potatoes in Sauce)	Colombia	7
Pasta Primavera	U.S.A.	134
Pasta Salad	U.S.A.	107
Polenta, Pesto and Tomatoes	U.S.A.	65
Semmelknodel (Dumplings)	Austria	139
Tabouli	Israel	151
Tsungtzu (Dumplings with Rice and Pork)	Taiwan	73
Ugali (Buttered Cornmeal)	Kenya	149
Uszka (Mushroom Ravioli)	Poland	155
Yorkshire Puddings	England	140

Zita's Rice	Hungary	104

MEATS

Australian Meat Pie	Australia	13
Blanquette d'Agneau (Lamb)	France	90
Bobotie (Beef Casserole)	South Africa	51
Carne de Asado (Roast Beef)	Peru	94
Chapchae (Beef Stir Fry)	Korea	116
Charcoal-Broiled Flank Steak	U.S.A.	86
Chicken and Pork Adabo	Philippines	75
Chiles en Nogada (Walnut Sauce)	Mexico	55
Chuletas de Cerdo en Salsa de Mango (Pork in Mango Sauce)	Colombia	5
Crown Roast of Pork with Apple-Sausage Dressing	U.S.A.	101
Empanadas de Horno (Meat Turnovers)	Chile	114
Feijoada (Black Bean Stew)	Brazil	80
Frikadeller (Meat Balls)	Denmark	160
Grilled Lamburgers	U.S.A.	109
Haggis, Neeps and Tatties	Scotland	11
Haggis in a Bowl	Scotland	11
Hapukapsas Sealihaga (Estonian Sauerkraut)	Estonia	27
Harvest Meal in a Milkcan	U.S.A.	100
Hungarian Pot Roast	Hungary	103
Lamb Kebabs	Australia	14
Lamb Pilau	Russia	45
Leg of Lamb with Stuffing	New Zealand	58
Khinkali (Meat Dumplings)	Georgia	127
Kiev Krucheniki	Ukraine	157
Musaqq'a (Eggplant Casserole)	Egypt	46
Patlecan Kebab (Eggplant)	Turkey	128
Pepper Steaks	England	141
Roast Beef and Yorkshire Puddings	England	140
Roast Pork	Czech Rep.	118
Rouladen mit Rotkohl (Meat Rolls with Red Cabbage)	Germany	124

Sate (Marinated Meats)	Indonesia	24
Sausage and Shrimp Jambalaya	Gulf States	160
Smoky Beef Brisket	U.S.A.	39
Steamed Short Ribs	Korea	115
Svickova (Beef in Cream Sauce)	Czech Rep.	119
Tailgatin' Hamburgers	U.S.A.	132
Tamales de Cerda (Pork Tamales with Vegetables)	Costa Rica	153
Tamatie Bredie (Lamb and Tomato Stew)	South Africa	52
Tsungtzu (Dumplings with Rice and Pork)	Taiwan	73
Veal and Ham Pie	U.S.A.	136
Veprona Pecene (Roast Pork)	Czech Rep.	118
Welsh Lamb with Honey	Wales	32

POULTRY AND GAME

Baked Chicken with Stuffing	Singapore	23
Chawan Mushi (Egg Custard with Chicken and Shrimp)	Japan	4
Chicken Curry	India	9
Chicken and Pork Adabo	Philippines	75
Chicken with Ajica Sauce	Georgia	126
Easy Israeli Chicken	Israel	151
Grandma Gilbert's Barbecued Chicken	U.S.A.	88
Lapin aux Raisins (Raisins Rabbit)	France	90
Oven-Fried Southern Chicken	U.S.A.	69
Martinigansl (Roast Goose)	Austria	138
Poule au Pot (Hen in a Pot)	France	89
Roast Turkey with Chestnut Stuffing	U.S.A.	142
Sate (Marinated Chicken)	Indonesia	24
Sour Cream Chicken Enchiladas	U.S.A.	40

SALADS

Curried Peach Salad	New Zealand	59
Ensalada Chilena	Chile	114
Fresh Fruit Cup	U.S.A.	133
Freezer Cole Slaw	U.S.A.	133
Frozen Pea Salad	U.S.A.	69
Gado Gado with Peanut Sauce	Indonesia	25
Kartulisalat (Potato Salad)	Estonia	29
Kumara Salad (Sweet Potatoes)	New Zealand	60
Marinated Potato Salad	U.S.A.	87
Papa a la Huancaina (Potatoes with Cream Sauce)	Peru	95
Pasta Primavera	U.S.A.	134
Pasta Salad	U.S.A.	107
Peedisalat (Beets and Caraway)	Estonia	29
Pineapple-Sour Cream Marshmellow Salad	U.S.A.	88
Raita (Vegetables in Yogurt)	India	9
Roasted Vegetable Salad	U.S.A.	102
Seenesalat (Mushroom Salad)	Estonia	29
Swedish Potato Salad	Sweden	78
Tabouli	Israel	151
Tahini Squash and Hummus	Israel	152
Texas Caviar	U.S.A.	41
Thüringer Kartoffelsalat (Potato Salad)	Germany	124
Wilted Spinach Salad	U.S.A.	18
Winter Vegetable Salad	Ukraine	158
Yusheng (Raw Fish Salad)	Singapore	22

SAUCES AND RELISHES

Ajica Sauce	Georgia	126
Baja (Walnut) Sauce	Georgia	127
Cocktail Sauce	Australia	15
Cranberry-Orange Relish	U.S.A.	143
Cucumber Sauce	Wales	33
Kimchee (Pickled Vegetables)	Korea	161
Mango Sauce	Colombia	6
Mustard Sauce	U.S.A.	137
Peanut Sauce	Indonesia	25